Re
r

# PRIVATE BEATSON'S WAR

# PRIVATE BEATSON'S WAR

## LIFE, DEATH AND HOPE ON THE WESTERN FRONT

A Diary of the Great War edited by
SHAUN SPRINGER AND
STUART HUMPHREYS

Foreword by
HENRY ALLINGHAM

Pen & Sword
**MILITARY**

First published in Great Britain in 2009 by
PEN & SWORD MILITARY
*an imprint of*
Pen & Sword Books Limited
47 Church Street
Barnsley
S. Yorkshire S70 2AS

ISBN 978 1 84884 082 9

A CIP catalogue record for this book
is available from the British Library

Typeset in Ehrhardt by S L Menzies-Earl

Printed and bound in England
by CPI


*Pen & Sword Books Ltd incorporates the imprints of*
Pen & Sword Aviation, Pen & Sword Maritime,
Pen & Sword Military, Wharncliffe Local History, Pen & Sword Select,
Pen & Sword Military Classics, Leo Cooper, Remember When,
Seaforth Publishing and Frontline Publishing


For a complete list of Pen & Sword titles please contact:
PEN & SWORD BOOKS LIMITED
47 Church Street, Barnsley, South Yorkshire, S70 2AS, England.
E-mail: enquiries@pen-and-sword.co.uk
Website: www.pen-and-sword.co.uk

# Contents

# List of Illustrations

**Maps**

**Plates**

For further notes and acknowledgements, see 'A Note
on the Photographs' on page 135.

*Section 1*

A young James Beatson with his mother, brother and sister.
(*Reproduced by courtesy of May Beatson*)
Beatson's father, John. (*Reproduced by courtesy of May Beatson*)
Private James Nicol Beatson. (*Reproduced by courtesy of May
Beatson*)
The first daily entry in Beatson's diary. (*Shaun Springer*)
Officers of the 9th Royal Scots at training camp in 1914. (*Stuart
Humphreys*)
The 9th Royal Scots resting during training exercises in 1914.
(*Reproduced by courtesy of the Imperial War Museum. Q51870*)
The 9th Royal Scots aboard HMT *Inventor*. (*Reproduced by
courtesy of Colonel R.P. Mason, Royal Scots Museum, Edinburgh*)
Argyll and Sutherland Highlanders wearing 'furries'. (*Reproduced by
courtesy of the Imperial War Museum. Q48957*)

# Foreword

## by Henry Allingham

Although there have been countless books written about the Great War of 1914–18, I read but few. It was only very late in my years that I realised the significance and, indeed, the value of such books, whose stories and events demanded to be told. Lest we forget.

No other generation has the right to ask that it be remembered. But this was a special and unique generation that was devastated, suffering almost a total eclipse, with its youth being put to the sword during the madness of a global war. The survivors then faced another conflict as they strove to bring up families and build a better life, laying the foundations for a prosperous Britain for future generations.

I am the oldest living survivor of that war. I am, indeed, the last man who was on active service confronting the enemy when peace was declared. To have been given the honour to append some words of my own as part of an introduction to this outstanding piece of writing truly humbled me. Here is a solitary tale of one man's war. An extraordinary exposition of life in the trenches, so brilliantly crafted. James Beatson's diary is the window through which we can look into the reality of war.

The definition of the word 'diary' is 'a book for making daily records'. What sets this diary apart from many others of the Great War is the unexpected profundity of Beatson's writing. On the face of it he was a simple plain-living army private caught up in the war. I stand in awe at his penmanship under dangerous and dreadful conditions – life expectancy was so low and for many the fear of death was often worse than death itself. James Beatson was, by my standards, a gifted young man whose powers of observation were remarkable. He seemed to know just where he was and what was expected of him, and was concerned about almost everything and everyone, including his enemy.

Contrast my war with that of Private Beatson. As a mechanic in the Royal Naval Air Service, my role was to bring aircraft up to the line and prepare them for combat duty to bomb and strafe the enemy; later I took part in the operations themselves, using the machine guns and dropping bombs. I was also responsible for the recovery of crashed aircraft. Mine was a faceless enemy. I had no hatred of him. During the last few months of the war I encountered streams of dejected German prisoners of war and I often thought to myself, 'poor devils'. I believed, as did James Beatson, that they were the same as us, with the same God, and I do believe that they had no desire to be at war.

I found that I had very little time to myself and I had no fixed abode. I was always kept on my toes doing what I was expected to do and having to make decisions on the hoof. This way of life cushioned me to some degree from worrying about what fate had in store – I was just too busy to worry about death. I saw awful death at first hand when pilots were trapped in the cockpit of a burning plane and I had to fight my guilt at my inability to help anyone. As there was only minimal supervision of my movements during periods when the weather curtailed flying, I regularly visited army units, including French and American camps, and was always made welcome – perhaps it was because I was a naval man without a ship or a telescope.

I came to Flanders complete with religious beliefs, having recently been confirmed in the Church of England. I can honestly say, unlike James Beatson, that my religion took a knock. My wife-to-be gave me a Bible, which I still treasure today. I read and re-read that Bible from cover to cover, not always for its religious content, but often as something to read. I was always an avid reader, but readable matter was scarce and hard to come by, much to my disappointment. My fellow comrades often chaffed me about my reading of the Bible, yet no one engaged me in a religious discussion.

I would love to have known James myself, but am pleased to have met him now through his diary and I readily extend my hand of friendship. The waste of this man's youthful and talented life reinforces my belief that war is responsible for far too many needless deaths to ever warrant glory.

> I saw a man long, long ago
> With a beard so white and hair like snow
> He passed me by that day
> I'm glad, so glad he passed my way.

Henry Allingham
January 2009

On 18 July 2009, shortly before the publication of this book, Henry died peacefully aged 113 at St Dunstan's, Brighton. Three years earlier, during a visit to the Somme, Henry had been asked how he wanted to be remembered. He answered: 'I don't. I want to be forgotten. Remember the others.' The editors are saddened by Henry's loss and hope that this book does justice to the memory of Henry, James and all their friends and comrades who sacrificed so much for their country and for future generations.

Henry supported 'Dark Horse Venture', a charity that encourages older people to get involved with a wide range of interests, including taking schoolchildren to the battlefields of Europe.

# Acknowledgements

I have had the privilege of being the temporary custodian of the diary of James Beatson since late 2006, when I purchased it at auction. I have transcribed the diary and written a few words, but the greater part of the research for this book has been completed by my co-editor, Stuart Humphreys – so any errors are entirely his doing. Having directed all potential litigants and complainants his way, I should, however, mention that without his selfless efforts in researching the diary it would never have reached publication.

The Great War Forum (http://1914-1918.invisionzone.com/forums) have been incredibly generous with their time and considerations. Their collective knowledge is peerless and I would recommend anyone with an unanswered question on the subject to visit the site. A kinder or more considerate bunch of enthusiasts you couldn't hope to meet.

I would also like to thank the Beatson family, especially James's niece, May Beatson, the daughter of his sister Bella, for her assistance, and William Beatson from the other side of the family. May's vibrant 87-year-old mind has provided almost all the facts about James's early life. The two charities that will enjoy all the royalties from this book, Starlight and St Dunstan's, have done all they can to assist us, for which I am grateful. Starlight Children's Foundation has succeeded through the years in bringing happiness into the lives of thousands of severely and terminally ill young people.

My deepest gratitude is extended to Denis Goodwin, the Chairman of the First World War Veterans Association. Denis was Henry Allingham's 'minder'. I met Henry in September 2008 when he launched his own marvellous book, *Kitchener's Last Volunteer: the Oldest Surviving Veteran of the Great War*, and was immediately struck by his incredible vitality. Henry, the oldest man in Europe and the last surviving founder member of the Royal Flying Corps, was 112 when we last met! With his typical open-hearted humour and that ever-present devilish twinkle in his deep blue eyes, he referred me to Denis, whom he called 'the Kid'. Denis was 82 and looked as much his age as I look 16. The two of them were a most remarkable pairing, and I consider myself privileged to have met them. I will never forget them.

Thanks must also go to Ed Maggs of Maggs Brothers Rare Books, Berkeley Square for hosting the book launch that will mark an agreeable start and finish to Stuart's and my 'fifteen minutes of fame' before we return to our day jobs.

Finally, my belated thanks to James Beatson himself for giving me such a gift in my life. To have my name associated with a book on the Great War was pretty much at the top of my 'wish list' and without James's wonderfully kind and erudite mind and exquisite penmanship this dream would never have come true.

*Shaun Springer*
Remembering Rifleman Maurice Springer,
King's Royal Rifle Corps
Killed in action, 4 November 1918


Nine months after being outbid at auction, I finally got round to contacting the buyer via the good offices of Dr Philip Errington at Sotheby's. To my great good fortune that buyer turned out to be Shaun Springer, an incredibly generous, larger-than-life character. He agreed at once that we should work together with the aim of publishing the diary for charitable purposes.

My second piece of good fortune during my research has been to make the acquaintance of so many kind people who have either a professional or an amateur interest in the Great War. Without fail they have given freely and selflessly of their time, effort and invaluable knowledge. For example, Tom Gordon was kind enough to provide me with a copy of the regimental war diary of the 9th Royal Scots from February 1915 to July 1916; several others we mention in 'A Note on the Photographs' on page 135.

St Dunstan's is the other charity that will benefit from the sales of this book. Over thirty members of the Royal Scots have been cared for by St Dunstan's since it opened its gates to blind ex-servicemen and women in 1915. Its Collections & Archives Manager, Roberta Hazan, has provided extremely useful advice to me throughout this project, for which I am grateful.

Publications like this often remark on the truly outstanding service provided by the Imperial War Museum, and this is no exception. I would like to thank Roderick Suddaby, Keeper of Documents, and all the staff at the Museum's documents, photographic, and newspaper and periodicals archives who diligently dealt with my enquiries, saving countless hours of what might otherwise have been fruitless endeavour.

For literary novices like Shaun and me, having Rupert Harding of Pen & Sword as our commissioning editor has been a godsend. The same applies to our publisher's design team in Barnsley, particularly Roni Wilkinson and Jon Wilkinson. Thanks must also go to the authors and broadcasters who kindly gave recommendations that we have used for publicity purposes.

I am pleased to acknowledge the excellent digital archive of the *Scotsman* (http://archive.scotsman.com) and thank Scotsman Publications Ltd for permission to quote from a number of articles that were published in that newspaper and the *Edinburgh Evening News*. Regarding copyright in general, we have made every effort to trace copyright holders; however, this has not always been possible.

Without the support and encouragement given by my wife Erika, this rather obsessive project would never have reached fruition. And thank you, the reader, for helping to keep alive the memory of James Beatson and those who fought and died with him in the Great War. In so doing, you have helped to support two charities, Starlight and St Dunstan's, of which James would surely have approved.

*Stuart Humphreys*
Remembering Private Edwin Charles Robert Barber,
Royal Welch Fusiliers
Killed in action at Ypres, 28 February 1917

# The Western Front
## Indicating Beatson's movements during 1915 and 1916

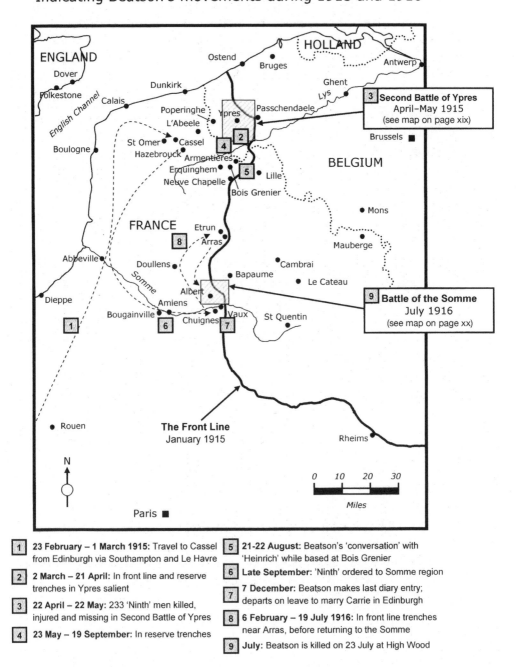

**ENGLAND**
Dover
Folkestone
Calais
*English Channel*
Boulogne

Ostend
Bruges
Dunkirk
Poperinghe
L'Abeele
Ypres
Passchendaele
St Omer   Cassel
Hazebrouck
Armentières
Erquinghem   Lille
Neuve Chapelle
Bois Grenier
**FRANCE**
Etrun
Arras
Doullens
Bapaume
Albert
Amiens
Bougainville
Chuignes   Vaux
St Quentin
Abbeville
*Somme*
Dieppe

**HOLLAND**
Antwerp
Ghent
*Lys*

**3** Second Battle of Ypres
April–May 1915
(see map on page xix)

Brussels ■

**BELGIUM**

Mons
Mauberge
Cambrai
Le Cateau

**9** Battle of the Somme
July 1916
(see map on page xx)

Rouen
The Front Line
January 1915
Rheims

N

Paris ■

0   10   20   30
Miles

**1** 23 February – 1 March 1915: Travel to Cassel from Edinburgh via Southampton and Le Havre

**2** 2 March – 21 April: In front line and reserve trenches in Ypres salient

**3** 22 April – 22 May: 233 'Ninth' men killed, injured and missing in Second Battle of Ypres

**4** 23 May – 19 September: In reserve trenches

**5** 21-22 August: Beatson's 'conversation' with 'Heinrich' while based at Bois Grenier

**6** Late September: 'Ninth' ordered to Somme region

**7** 7 December: Beatson makes last diary entry; departs on leave to marry Carrie in Edinburgh

**8** 6 February – 19 July 1916: In front line trenches near Arras, before returning to the Somme

**9** July: Beatson is killed on 23 July at High Wood

# The Second Battle of Ypres
## Movements of the 9th Royal Scots during the Battle

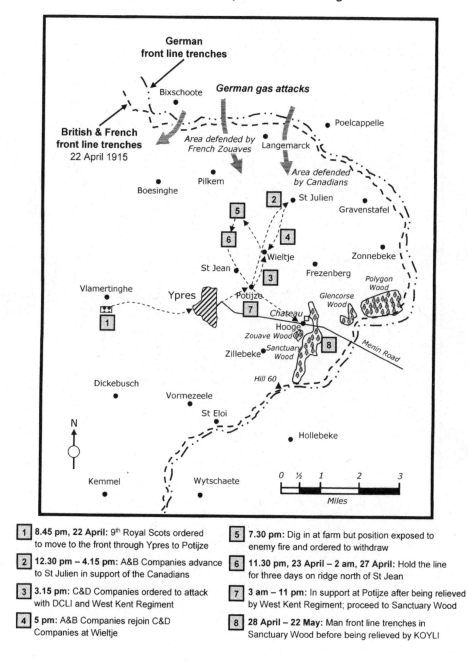

# Battle of the Somme

Beatson's death at High Wood, 23 July 1916

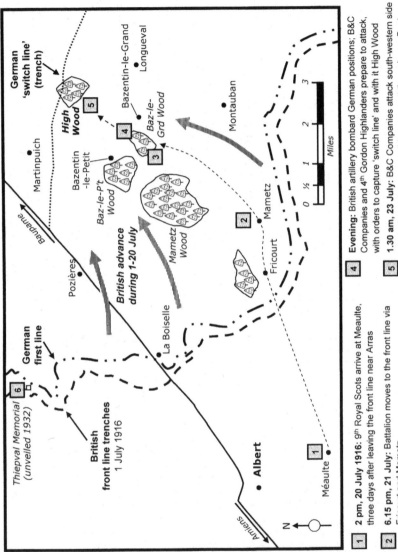

1. **2 pm, 20 July 1916:** 9th Royal Scots arrive at Meaulte, three days after leaving the front line near Arras

2. **6.15 pm, 21 July:** Battalion moves to the front line via Fricourt and Mametz

3. **22 July:** A&D Companies in front line trenches; B&C Companies in reserve trenches at south-west edge of Bazentin-le-Grand Wood

4. **Evening:** British artillery bombard German positions; B&C Companies and 4th Gordon Highlanders prepare to attack, with orders to capture 'switch line' and with it High Wood

5. **1.30 am, 23 July:** B&C Companies attack south-western side of wood, but German machine guns cut them down. Beatson and 73 fellow men of the Ninth are killed, 100 wounded.

6. **Present day:** Beatson commemorated at Thiepval Memorial

# Editors' Note

What you are about to read is the moving, very personal story of an extraordinary man living in extraordinary times; a young man destined to die, like so many of his generation, on the Western Front in the First World War, the 'Great War'. This is the diary of James Beatson, a member of B Company of the 9th Battalion, Royal Scots, a territorial force affectionately known as the 'Dandy Ninth'. Beatson was a private when he started writing his diary, and without disregarding his subsequent promotions to lance-corporal and then corporal, we have tended to refer to him as Private Beatson throughout.

Beatson's diary was owned by his niece May Beatson, and during the ninety years after it was written she proudly showed it first to her children and then to her grandchildren. A great deal of publicity surrounded the diary's auction in December 2006 at Sotheby's, London. Dr Gabriel Heaton, Sotheby's manuscript specialist and an expert on wartime diaries, described it thus:

> In terms of its detail and the empathy he shows for his fellow human beings, the villagers who were having their homes destroyed and for the Germans he was fighting, it is amazing, and that's what makes it special. It is one of the most moving documents I have seen in my career. It is a powerful and emotive witness to one of the darkest episodes in European military history.

Extracts were widely published at the time of the auction in national and Scottish regional newspapers and on the internet. This, however, is the first time that the diary has been published in its entirety, fully transcribed and edited.

Unfortunately, the second volume of the diary, which Beatson would undoubtedly have kept upon his return to the Western Front in late December 1915, presumably lies with him to this day in the Somme mud. His body probably remains where it fell, cut down by German machine guns as the Ninth went 'over the top' before sunrise one July morning in 1916 in the first weeks of the Battle of the Somme. He was killed three days before his 24th birthday.

Although we have endeavoured to ensure that historical references are factually correct, this is far from being a comprehensive military history. For those wishing to read more about the period covered by Beatson's diary, we recommend the texts listed in the bibliography, particularly Lyn Macdonald's seminal *1915, The Death of Innocence*, which perfectly encompasses the period and includes verbatim experiences of other Royal Scots.

In bringing Beatson's diary to the attention of a wider audience, and in so doing raising funds for our chosen charities, Starlight and St Dunstan's, we hope we have done justice to this incredible man, his loving family, his gallant comrades in the Royal Scots, and indeed the brave soldiers on all sides who fought and fell in the Great War.

Finally, if anyone has any further information on James Beatson and the events described in his diary, we would be delighted to hear from you via our publishers.

Shaun Springer and Stuart Humphreys
July 2009

# Introduction

## The Diary after 90 Years

The diary spans the period from Private Beatson's arrival in France in February 1915 through to December 1915 when he prepared to return to Edinburgh on a week's leave to marry his sweetheart, bakery assistant Caroline Wight. He was 23, she 19. And it is to 'Carrie' that Beatson dedicated his diary:

> When I started this diary I intended addressing my remarks to the shade of my sweetheart, but I was led from the base narrative of events. Love and war are not fit to be mentioned together; love makes us friends with the world, war violates us. Only God understands us . . .

During this period he experienced the best and the worst of times. He enjoyed the comradeship of his fellow soldiers and the adventure of travel in a foreign land, especially the relaxed atmosphere of cafés and *éstaminets*, the fragile peace and beauty of Belgian villages and the fields of Flanders, which he described as 'A very pretty countryside to spend a holiday in, on a bicycle.' Yet after less than two months in Belgium, he and his comrades suffered the trauma of the Second Battle of Ypres: 'Passing . . . along the Menin Road into Ypres, we saw the hideous ruins, the result of the last bombardment. Words haven't been coined to describe the desolation.' This offensive was the first on the Western Front in which the German army deployed poison gas: 'Stink bombs, bursting and sickening us with poisonous fumes and inflaming our eyes.'

Private Beatson's descriptions of daily life on the Western Front are sometimes humorous, often poignant, always eloquent. They are coloured with biblical themes and literary references taken from, amongst others, works by George Bernard Shaw, John Milton, his fellow Scot Robert Louis Stevenson, the continental writers Emile Zola and Honoré de Balzac, and the Americans Henry James and Jerome K. Jerome; he also quotes the Belgian poet Leon Montenaeken. He could read French and was conversant with the most up-to-date aspects of science, as illustrated by his reference on 21 August to the emerging theory of nuclear physics: 'O wonderful and intricate world and universe in which, if an atom of matter were destroyed, the whole would tumble to pieces.'

Beatson's diary comprises 149 pages written in purple and blue ink in an unruled, government-issue notebook. It is written in a neat and careful hand throughout; in over 20,000 words there are no more than half a dozen spelling mistakes or crossings out. From the first diary entry to the last there is barely a single crooked line. Given that on occasion Beatson was writing in the front line – sometimes under direct bombardment from enemy shellfire – how he managed to do so is testament to the care and attention he bestowed upon his work.

The diary is prefaced with a sombre note beginning 'In the event of my death . . .' on page 1. As with soldiers throughout the ages, superstition was rife at the front, and Beatson duly left page 13 blank. The last entry is on page 81, pages 79, 80 and 82 being absent. It seems unlikely that a man of Beatson's exactitude and evident pride in his work would have allowed his diary to end so perfunctorily, and so it is reasonable to assume that more entries were recorded and later excised from the diary.

Curiously, in the preface Beatson recorded the regimental numbers of the two men to whom he entrusted his diary, William Swan and Cecil Valentine, as 2288 and 2355 respectively, rather than the correct 2283 and 2358. These small transposition errors we can perhaps attribute to a certain nervousness as he started writing his diary while crossing the Channel to France aboard a crowded cattle ship.

The question must be addressed as to when the diary was penned. The lack of errors and corrections is remarkable for a narrative of such emotional depth and profundity of thought. Many Great War diaries were rewritten during periods of leave or formed from recollections after the war. The latter, alas, was not an option in the case of Beatson. The only substantial period of time available to him to have written the diary at a later date was when he returned on leave in December 1915 to wed his sweetheart. One imagines he had more pleasurable pastimes to pursue during his week-long honeymoon than to immerse himself in the all-too-real dreadfulness of the Western Front to which he was shortly to return.

The evidence that the diary was written on the dates stated seems overwhelming. On two occasions Beatson's text indicates a drawing or diagram to be referred to by the reader. Logic suggests that a rewritten diary would include these illustrations or at least leave space for them to be inserted later on; there are neither drawings nor spacings present. More pertinent is what might be called the 'tipsy' entry for 9 June. This is the only page where Beatson's writing goes somewhat awry. With its crossings out and sloping lines this particular entry is best understood if you imagine him merrily slurring his words at the end of a night out before finishing off the entry the next morning when he has slept off the effects of the previous night. But most telling of all is the entry for 10 May, when he was writing under direct shell fire while 'standing to'. The very words quiver and tremble. The page is the grubbiest in the whole diary, as if mud and debris have been dusted from it. Indeed, it seems the diary itself bears the memory of the bombardment about which James was writing as he sheltered from its random terror. Finally, the diary is of standard military issue and size, the sort commonly possessed by both ordinary ranks and officers.

A few comments about our transcription of the diary. The minimal editing has been limited to amending hyphenated words to provide their modern usage, for example 'country-side' becomes 'countryside', and to changing some of Beatson's overabundant commas into full stops. Whereas Beatson wrote each day's entry in continuous form in order to save space, we have incorporated paragraphs into the narrative. We have also included brief introductory notes at the start of each month, italicised in order to differentiate them from the diary's entries. Once the diary begins, all the words are exactly as Beatson penned them except for the editors' insertions, all of which are in italics. Also, to guide the reader through the chronology of events, we have added sub-headings to the daily entries as well as noting the location of B Company and, hence, of Beatson at the time.

Much discussion went on regarding notes and insertions. Overall, we felt that inserting an italicised note [*thus*] or a footnote, where this was necessary to explain a word or phrase Beatson had used, would assist the reader's continuity of reading. Longer explanatory notes and cross-references to sources have been included in the endnotes.

### Beatson's Family and Upbringing

Born in Leith, Edinburgh on 26 July 1892 to John, a labourer, and Elizabeth ('Eliza'), a domestic servant, James Nicol Beatson was the eldest of nine children. They were not a wealthy family, though John's brother, James's Uncle William, lived with his even larger family of eleven children in a big house on one of Edinburgh's smartest streets. John himself was the eldest of eleven children, with Uncle William the second in line. Aside from James's twenty aunts and uncles, he had a further thirty-five close relatives from the previous generation on his father's side alone. And most of them had children named James, William or John, a fact that makes researching the Beatson family history and military enrolment records a less than straightforward affair.

Uncle William became a prominent member of the United Free Church and an important dignitary of the City of Edinburgh. John, on the other hand, was ever the life and soul of the party, always buying another round to keep it going. Family legend has it that William and John argued heatedly over money, not surprisingly, and eventually severed all ties between their respective families. They were to remain divided for over a century.

James, John's eldest son, enjoyed an education sufficiently full to enable him to article as a civil engineer. Isabella, the second eldest child, is the 'Bella' to whom James so often refers in his diary. But James and Bella were to be set apart from their siblings. While their Uncle William was buying the streets of Edinburgh, John was paving them, and a paver's salary did not stretch to feeding and clothing, let alone educating, nine children. So James and Bella were packed off to live with their grandparents at Bonar Bridge up in the highlands of Scotland. There, from the ages of 8 and 7 respectively, James and Bella attended Larachan School in Fife, a school financed by the great philanthropist Andrew Carnegie.

Larachan was a small school teaching no more than thirty children spread over three classes, with five dormitories for those far from home. James and Bella were, however, fortunate enough to live locally with their grandfather, James Beatson senior. He was a plasterer, and evidently a good one since he was able to raise eleven children. Demand for such skills had been high in Edinburgh during the expansive 1860s and 1870s, and no doubt James senior put something away for a rainy day.

Set in the hills 40 miles west of Inverness, the grey stone gothic mansion that formerly housed Larachan School is today a private residence. It was sold for nearly £½ million in late 2006, and one imagines the heating facilities have been significantly upgraded in the intervening hundred years. Nevertheless, for James and Bella it was a good school with dedicated teachers and comparatively good funding. Many years later it would hold fond memories for Bella, who recalled, more than anything, the freedom of thought and space. What better school-time memory could one wish for?

Bella was fetched out to work in the local croft when her education was deemed complete at the wizened age of 12, while James continued his studies until he was 16. They enjoyed their childhood and teenage years and Bella would later recollect warm, close and tender days of security and love. Above all, she would remember the stories read to her and her brother by their grandfather, and the hours passed reading absolutely everything they could lay their hands on. Both brother and sister had voracious appetites for information: local and national news, literature, in fact anything at all. Their grandfather joined the chase with enthusiasm and the three of them would while away the long highland nights huddled round the latest book or periodical. It is perhaps not surprising that one of Bella's few personal effects still in the family's possession is the top prize awarded for English at Larachan School in 1905 – it is a dictionary, worn and well-thumbed.

Facts are few and far between for James's later adolescence. We know that Bella continued to work in the croft. Family history records that James went into higher education, and after receiving a scholarship he qualified as a civil engineer and found employment with Edinburgh City Council's Valuation Office. At the outbreak of war he was still completing his apprenticeship with them, most likely undertaking surveys.

James's mother, Eliza, died of pulmonary phthisis (tuberculosis) or 'consumption' in 1911, just a year after the birth of her last child, George. And so maternal duties fell into Bella's lap, now at the tender age of 18.

James's father, John, was clearly none too diligent with his pennies. Though he played a mean tune on the ivories and was ever the hale and hearty foreman of the local working men's club, his limitless optimism never quite manifested itself materially. James, in all likelihood, found the road taken by his wealthy and influential Uncle William a more secure one upon which to tread. As can be seen from the photograph of John reproduced in this book, he was nonetheless a large and proud man. Strong as an ox and as gentle as feather-down he may have been, but he was devastated by the death of his wife from the 'wasting disease' and then crushed by the separation of his family. His love for James and Bella was boundless, his pride in James's academic success perhaps marred only by the fact that he had not played any significant part in helping his son achieve it.

In early August 1914 war was declared. Now aged 22, James was in Edinburgh, working in the Valuation Office, and courting his sweetheart 'Carrie', baker's shop assistant Caroline Wight. On 19

August he answered Kitchener's call to arms and enlisted in the 9th Royal Scots. The record of Beatson's army medical survives and attests to him being 5ft 6¹/₄in tall and weighing 140¹/₂lb, pretty much the average height and weight of recruits at the time. As a member of a territorial force, he had to sign an agreement to serve outside the United Kingdom, which he duly did on 28 August.

Beatson was not the only member of his family to enlist; indeed, the mightily large Beatson clan might almost have formed its own battalion. John joined the Royal Scots alongside his son James and numerous other members of the family, including James's younger brother Donald, known as 'Don'. Other family members helped fill the swelling ranks of various noble regiments, including the Camerons and the Argyll & Sutherland Highlanders.

Miraculously, nearly all of the immediate family survived the war. Only James and two of his cousins died: one was killed on the Somme during the German army's 1918 Spring Offensive while serving with the 13th Battalion, Royal Scots, while one of Uncle William's sons in the Argyll & Sutherland Highlanders died of wounds in October 1915, also in France. John was 44 years old when he joined up and so served in a 'provisional' battalion; he did not see front-line service, though he rose through the ranks to become, not surprisingly, a pipe major. Bizarrely, Don, having survived many of the major Western Front campaigns during the war, returned home only to perish a few years later in a vat of molten steel at the foundry where he worked.

### Beatson's Passion

And that is all we know of James Beatson from the record books and family lore. Who was James Beatson? What do his words tell us about him? What can the diary, into which he poured his most precious thoughts, tell us about Beatson to give an insight into this young, love-smitten patriot?

By the start of the war he was a thoroughly educated young man, deeply religious and extremely well versed in the literature of the time. Without doubt he was a fun-loving lad. His time behind the lines was filled with appreciation of life's small treasures and the joy of simply being alive. He was no great drinker but certainly no teetotaller; though he participated in the daily rum ration, it was more to enjoy the inner warmth generated in the bitter winter winds of early 1915 than to appreciate its questionable vintage: 'The notorious tot of rum is served each night but I used it only on Wednesday and then only watered down.'

We also know he revelled in his nights and days 'on the tiles' and, as already mentioned, one page of his diary reads almost diagonally, attesting to his lack of puritanical abstinence. He also enjoyed the benefits of a ready wit, having known from his earliest days the dry, sardonic humour that only Edinburgh can breed, not to mention having a larger-than-life father with a ready quip for every contingency. His diary is littered with amusing insights into everything and everyone he encounters. His jovial asides on the French are still reflected by humorous commentators today, as indeed are his self-deprecating barbs at the British: 'We British are game to the last, but damned stupid at times.'

For British James Beatson was; he was Scottish first, of course, but British to the end. He was rightly proud of his regiment and joyously trumpeted its achievements and accolades. The Royal Scots were a 'reliable' regiment. They did what was asked of them, whatever the cost; by February 1915 they boasted a well-deserved reputation among the Army's top brass. During Beatson's time with them, not a single member of his battalion was court-martialled. And no matter how much Beatson railed against the other Scottish regiments' behaviour, they could do no wrong on the field of battle. Yet whenever he speaks of any of his traits or those of his comrades that are of a nationalistic nature, he refers to them as British characteristics rather than as English, Scottish, Welsh or Irish. But as with any soldier of any age, his greatest allegiance and love were reserved for his brothers-in-arms, and no pain was greater than the loss of a comrade.

Alick, dear, dear Alick, staunch and true, generous, open as the day. I loved you as a brother and would gladly have given myself

in your place. Never will I meet your like again, never will I
forget you, never will I mourn you as I ought. May God count
me worthy to meet you again, dear, dear brother of mine, Alick.

The two lines that follow the above entry have very slight water stains
on them, smudging the ink. We can never know whether the stains
were caused by Beatson's tears, but they are the only such marks in the
diary.

The most common thread throughout Beatson's narrative is his
questioning but pure belief in God. He does not divulge his church
but it is likely he followed his family's roots and was from the United
Free Church, as were most of the Royal Scots. For James, God took
no side except for humanity. Can the timeless question of God's
interest in man's constant conflicts be more eloquently phrased than
in the following diary entry?

Good Friday! Has mankind any heart or brain? Are we too
utterly dense and blind to the greatest good? Then well may
God give us up to a brutish death at our brother's hands. But
no! As we are made in the image of God I believe we're doing
His will in crushing this big bellied military force. But again, the
Kaiser claims the alliance of God sincerely or insincerely. Or is
this God dispassionately feeding His earth with men?

'God pity us' is a phrase James used often when his despair of
mankind reached limits we cannot today imagine. And James sought
pity for all, not just for the Allied troops. For this young patriot, God
was for all men of whatever persuasion or nationality. He asks God to
pity the enemy as often as he asks it for himself and his comrades:
'"Our Father which art in Heaven". Scots, French, Germans,
Austrians, Russians and the rest, return to "our" Mother Earth,
groaning and cursing.'

Although he might comment caustically on Catholic symbolism,
James nevertheless embraced Catholicism's love of God; on arriving
at an abandoned and desecrated abbey he noted:

Pictures on all sides show ghastly hearts dripping with blood and flaming, encircled with a wreath of roses. The endless variation on that theme is depressing and the thought of girls spending the bloom of youth contemplating such is repulsive to my mind. But I found here a letter written by a girl in Coventry to the Right Hon. Lady Abbess which breathed with religion, the sincerity of which was touching.

Indeed, God is everywhere in James's diary. He thanks him for a bath as wholeheartedly as he does for his life. James saw God in everything from the horrific to the idyllic: 'Occasionally a barge with sails big-bellied with God's own breezes glides slowly by.' After surviving the first major gas attack in the history of warfare and following a week of unimaginably intense activity, stress and battle, James concluded a remarkable entry by combining his faith with his humorous nature and his good-spirited optimism: 'Never mind, God's in His Heaven. Keep looking up.'

### 'Heinrich' – His Enemy, His Friend

The most remarkable feature of Beatson's diary is the unique 'friendship' formed with a dead Prussian officer known only as 'Heinrich', whose own diary was found in a captured trench and published by the British for propaganda reasons. Despite the horrors of life on the Western Front – the sudden, shocking loss of dear friends and comrades, the incessant shelling, the waterlogged trenches and plagues of 'slow, fat, waddling' rats – Beatson developed a strong, binding empathy with his erstwhile enemy.

The concept of 'enemy as friend' or 'enemy as brother' is found in a number of writings from the Great War, certainly more so than in any other conflict before or since, and is alluded to in Henry Allingham's Foreword to this book. The two longest entries in the diary are the passages written on 21 and 22 August 1915, where Beatson describes his reading of Heinrich's diary; they display an emotional resonance that bears comparison with the Great War poets. Of Heinrich's involvement in hand-to-hand fighting, he wrote:

Astonishing moments in battle when a man suddenly appears before you. A man you have never seen before yet who, in a flash, suddenly becomes everything to you. He is the man coming to kill you yet you do not hate him in the least. Yet you take in every detail of his face; remember the face of a boy of eighteen or so, white, with teeth exposed and haggard eyes, like a runner in the last stage of an exhausting race. His eyes were on you yet they seemed unseeing, though like a furious mechanical figure, he was about to pitchfork you aside with his bayonet when your revolver did for him.

Later in the war, in his poem 'Strange Meeting', described by Siegfried Sassoon as his 'passport to immortality', Wilfred Owen would describe thus the meeting of the ghosts of two dead soldiers, one British, the other German:

> Yet also there encumbered sleepers groaned,
> Too fast in thought or death to be bestirred.
> Then, as I probed them, one sprang up, and stared
> With piteous recognition in fixed eyes,
> Lifting distressful hands, as if to bless.
> And by his smile, I knew that sullen hall,
> By his dead smile I knew we stood in Hell.

And, like Beatson and Heinrich, Owen's protagonists cease to be enemies and they rise beyond mortal conflict:

> I am the enemy you killed, my friend.
> I knew you in this dark: for so you frowned
> Yesterday through me as you jabbed and killed.
> I parried; but my hands were loath and cold.
> Let us sleep now . . .

As Beatson read Heinrich's diary he began to change, identifying more and more with this German soldier. In a telling slip in this passionate piece of prose, Beatson so completely identified himself with 'Captain von H' that he used the word 'I' in place of 'you': 'Then the great laughing face of a heavy man of the innkeeper type, jovial, yet seeming petrified, laughing yet a thousand leagues from laughter and when I trod over it to get beyond, laughing no doubt still.'

That he made such a slip while analysing Heinrich underlines the affinity he felt for his enemy. And Beatson's own haunting final homily to Heinrich and the hope it inspired among all the death and destruction provides a fitting tribute to his compassionate nature:

> Are you dead Heinrich? I know you would die bravely and quietly. Fate has labelled you Prussian and me British, but I would do a long pilgrimage to lay flowers on the grave that holds your body. It is a perfect Sunday afternoon. The blue sky is dappled with white puffs of shrapnel smoke; with that exception there is nothing of war.

## Beatson's War in Context – 1915

*The Western Front and the Ypres Salient*

Britain's entry into the war in August 1914 had been precipitated by Germany's invasion of neutral Belgium. Based largely on the Schlieffen Plan devised more than a decade earlier, the German strategy had been to bypass the heavily fortified French border towns, instead moving at speed through Belgium with a view to capturing Paris before the French army could be properly mobilised. In the event, stronger than expected resistance from the Belgian army – what Heinrich refers to as the 'Belgian joggle' – and the combined forces of the French army and the British Expeditionary Force (BEF) at the battles of Le Cateau, Mons, the Marne and Ypres prevented the Germans from succeeding in their objective.

Rather than being 'over by Christmas', as had been generally expected by the populations of all the combatant nations, the war on the Western Front continued into 1915, with both sides literally entrenched along a 400-mile line, as the crow flies, stretching from the

English Channel to the Swiss Alps. The winter of 1914/15 was so cold, wet and miserable that it was labelled 'the wet winter' by the Germans. On occasion temperatures plummeted to a bone-numbing –15°C.

At the First Battle of Ypres on 22 November 1914 the BEF had successfully defended the ancient Belgian town, thus stopping the German army in its 'race to the sea' and denying it access to the Channel ports of Dunkirk, Calais and Boulogne. These were vital to supplying the Allied forces with men and equipment, in addition to providing exit ports for the BEF should the Germans succeed in splitting the French from the British forces. East of Ypres the Allies held part of the line that extended several miles into German territory, a salient that was, by definition, liable to enemy attack from three sides. The defence of the Ypres salient was the task that awaited Private Beatson and the 9th Royal Scots as they made their way to the front line.

The first major land battle of 1915 on the Western Front took place at Neuve Chapelle in northern France. Between 10 and 13 March the British attempted to break through the German line, but the attack failed at a cost of 13,000 British soldiers dead, injured or missing.

Although marked by countless acts of heroism and bravery, May was a disastrous month for Britain and her allies; indeed, it was arguably one of the worst of the entire war. Just nine months into the conflict both sides still believed a 'quick' victory could be theirs, but it was the Germans who went on the offensive following the gas attack at Ypres in late April. The Second Battle of Ypres raged from 22 April until 25 May, as the Germans attacked and pushed back the defences on the north-eastern side of the salient. For most of the battle Beatson and the 9th Royal Scots manned front-line trenches near Hooge, suffering heavy casualties: 32 killed, 193 wounded. As the fighting continued, Sanctuary Wood acquired a rather ironic meaning, and later in the war an officer would write: 'Of the terrible and horrible scenes I have seen in the war, Sanctuary Wood is the worst . . . Dante in his worst imaginings never conceived a like.' The fighting here is described in more detail later in this Introduction.

On 9 May the Allies attempted a counter-attack. The French attacked at Vimy Ridge and despite heavy casualties achieved some limited success, the Germans being forced to retreat, albeit to more strongly fortified trenches. On the same day the British launched a disastrous attempt to capture Aubers Ridge, opposite Fromelles and La Bassée. Unfortunately, many – perhaps most – of the shells used in the initial 'softening up' of the German lines were either ineffective – too much shrapnel, not enough explosive – or defective; some were even filled by one fraudulent manufacturer with sawdust rather than gunpowder. This inadequate artillery bombardment failed to have much impact on the German defences, leaving the advancing British and Indian troops exposed to merciless machine-gun fire. To make matters worse, much worse, not only did British artillery shells start to fall short of their intended targets, but retreating soldiers with German prisoners were mistaken for the enemy and so were fired upon by the British trenches. This deadly three-way cross-fire – a combination of the relentless German fire and what is now euphemistically called 'friendly fire' – decimated whole battalions of Sherwood Foresters and Northamptonshire Yeomanry. A few days later *The Times* published General Sir John French's damning indictment: 'British soldiers died last week on Aubers Ridge because the British Army is short of shells.' Ironically, the shortage of British shells had its roots in skilled industrial workers leaving their factories to join Kitchener's New Army.

After the Second Battle of Ypres there was a brief period without any major offensives. But there were, of course, no truly quiet days for the British forces and by September the largest artillery war ever fought on European soil was in full flow around Beatson's old environs, as he regularly remarks. As the month drew to a close the Battle of Loos opened with a successful advance on Hill 70 by the Guards, only for them to lose it the next day at the cost of the majority of the division. This British offensive was designed to support the larger French attack launched in the Argonne and Champagne/Artois regions, which culminated in the capture of

Vimy Ridge. In October the French continued their vigorous campaign in Champagne with limited success, and Germany launched a formidable offensive against Loos on 8 October, suffering horrendous casualties in the process, although the numbers were small in comparison to their losses in the east.

### The Eastern Front

Simultaneously, the Germans were engaged in an equally deadly struggle on their Eastern Front, fighting alongside the Austro-Hungarian Empire (together with Bulgaria and the Ottoman Empire, the 'Central Powers') against Serbia and pre-Revolutionary Russia. At this stage the conflict was essentially still a European war. Although there was some fighting in parts of colonial Africa, the greatest enemy there was disease rather than machine guns or artillery. It would only become a truly global conflict with the entry of the United States into the war two years later.

The Austro-Hungarians and Russians fought a series of bloody battles in Galicia, a region today divided between Poland and the Ukraine. Beatson records how 'We heard the Huns shouting and singing opposite us . . . over the fall of Lemberg.' This town, formerly Lwow in Poland and now Lviv in the Ukraine, would in fact change hands several times during the war, on this occasion in late June 1915 being recaptured by the Austro-Hungarians.

In May the Austro-Hungarians and Germans launched a massive assault against the Russians in the Carpathian mountains. Starting with a barrage of almost three-quarters of a million shells, the attack was an overwhelming success, tens of thousands of Russian soldiers being killed or taken prisoner. With the Russian army in retreat, the Austrians wanted to explore the opportunity to sue for peace with Russia, much to the chagrin of the Germans, who remained convinced that victory on the Western Front would be within reach once the Russians were broken in the east. They were confident they could destroy the Russian army and capture vast tracts of agricultural land in the east to complement the anticipated gain of industrial towns in the west. So the fighting on the Eastern Front continued.

By September massive armies were being moved around like pawns on the Eastern Front, where Tsar Nicholas II had now assumed supreme command of the Russian forces. This was an ill-advised move that hastened the exit of Russia as an effective ally eighteen months later. At the end of August Beatson remarks on the defeats inflicted on Russia. However, the Tsar was immediately rewarded in September with a string of minor victories that demonstrated, in his view, God's approval of his 'promotion'.

*Gallipoli and Events in Turkey*
In October 1914 Turkey had entered the war as an ally of the Central Powers. Six months later, on 25 April 1915, Allied troops landed at Gallipoli. This ill-fated campaign, inspired by Winston Churchill, First Lord of the Admiralty, had many, perhaps too many, objectives. These included: defending the strategically important Suez Canal; targeting the Turkish capital, Constantinople (now Istanbul); and opening up a second front against the Central Powers, or at least supporting the Russian army on the Eastern Front. The landings followed an extensive, but ultimately ineffective, British naval bombardment of the Turkish forts guarding the Dardanelles Straits, and were delayed by disagreements within the Admiralty.

In the event, the Turkish defenders overcame the initial surprise of the landings, and the Allies were unable to gain a proper foothold. After grievous loss of life on both sides, not least among the gallant Australian and New Zealand Army Corps (Anzacs), the Allies were forced to withdraw. Although the evacuation, which was finally completed in January 1916 without further heavy loss of life, was a relative success, the assault on Gallipoli was an unmitigated disaster. Yet in August 1915 Beatson refers to 'the brilliant generalship at the Dardanelles': clearly 'spin' is not just a modern-day phenomenon.

Later in the year the first reports surfaced of atrocities being committed against the Armenians in eastern Turkey. This was deemed so serious a matter that it was shortly thereafter discussed in the House of Lords, and remains a source of debate among the international community to the present day.

*Naval Warfare in the North Sea*

Whereas the Gallipoli campaign was a combined sea and land assault, a number of sea battles were also fought. In the North Sea the Royal Navy, long the dominant naval power of the world, faced the emerging German High Seas Fleet.

On 24 January 1915, a month before the Royal Scots' departure for the Western Front, the Battle of Dogger Bank took place in the North Sea between British and German naval forces. Despite the superior fire-power of the British fleet's dreadnoughts, there was no outright victor, but the result was that Germany's High Seas Fleet would remain largely confined to its north German bases until the Battle of Jutland in May 1916. Any skirmishes in the Baltic and North Seas in the meantime were inconclusive. So, when in August 1915 Beatson was cheered by news of 'the splendid naval victory in the Baltic', we must again thank the efficiency of British propaganda.

*The U-boat Threat in the Atlantic*

In the Atlantic German submarines engaged in their deadly pursuit of Allied and American military, commercial and civilian shipping. Neither the convoy system nor sonar were yet in use to counter the ever-increasing tonnage being sunk. On 7 May 1915 the German submarine *U-20* torpedoed and sank the British ocean liner *Lusitania* off the southern coast of Ireland as she neared the end of her Atlantic crossing from New York to Liverpool. Thomas Henry Hall Caine, a best-selling novelist to whom Beatson refers in his diary, wrote a series of flag-waving articles for the *Daily Telegraph* which were published in 1915 as a collected work entitled *The Drama of 365 Days: Scenes in the Great War*. In this passage he captures the prevailing mood of the British public in describing the sinking as 'the crowning horror of Germany's barbarities':

> When the *Lusitania* was sunk in broad daylight . . . it was because our brother man, in the bitterness of his heart and the cruelty of his fear, had been bent on committing wilful murder.

What is the present state of the soul of the person who perpetrated that crime? Can he excuse himself on the ground that he was obeying orders . . . When he first saw the great ship sailing up in the sunshine, its decks crowded out with peaceful passengers, and he rose like a murderer out of his hiding-place in the bowels of the sea, what were his feelings with which he ordered the torpedo to be fired?

Hall Caine ended the article with Tacitus's well-worn verdict: 'The character of the Germans shows a terrible mixture of ferocity and infamy. It is a people born to lie.'

Like the British government, Hall Caine hoped that the sinking of the *Lusitania* would bring the United States, still neutral at this point, into the war. It certainly created a diplomatic crisis between Germany and the United States: of the 1,200 civilian passengers who drowned, 128 were American citizens. Ultimately, the unrestricted U-boat threat to its own commercial shipping interests compelled the United States to enter the war in 1917, providing the overwhelming force that helped break the German spirit, end the stalemate of trench warfare and defeat Germany.

*Italy Joins the Allies*
On 23 May 1915 Italy joined the war on the side of the Allies by declaring war on the Austro-Hungarian empire. Facing an enemy that had the benefit of strong Alpine mountain defences, the Italians went on to suffer proportionately the gravest losses of any of the combatant nations, losing some 650,000 military dead, with the total of dead and wounded exceeding two million out of a population of just over thirty-five million.

*The 'Home Front'*
On the Home Front the initial threat of invasion had receded, but there was a great fear of air attacks by Germany's fleet of thirty rigid airships, known as 'Zeppelins', against which the British had no effective defence. The first Zeppelin air raid on British soil took place

at Kings Lynn on 19 January 1915; four people were killed. Three months later Ipswich and Bury St Edmunds were bombed. The psychological effect of these raids is often underestimated, overshadowed as they are by the Blitz of the Second World War, but certainly the anxiety they generated among the population far outweighed their physical effect. Death raining down from the sky over civilian centres was the stuff from which nightmares were made. Kaiser Wilhelm was, however, initially wary of bombing non-military targets in London and, indeed, Britain's First Sea Lord, Admiral Fisher, issued blood-curdling warnings of the reprisals that would follow any such attack. In late May the Kaiser changed his mind and on the night of 31 May Zeppelin *LZ38* bombed various targets in east London. But it was not until 8 September 1915, over a year after the start of the war, that central London was attacked, a raid by Zeppelin *L13* leaving twenty-six civilians dead. Eventually the Royal Flying Corps acquired aircraft able to tackle the Zeppelins and this, combined with a lack of conviction on the German side about this form of warfare, meant that by mid-1917 the threat from the air was over.

On 22 May 1915 over 100 sailors drowned when the German submarine *U-21* torpedoed HMS *Triumph* off the Dardanelles coast. On the same day 214 soldiers and 12 civilians were killed and 246 others injured in the disastrous Gretna rail crash, the worst ever railway accident in Britain. It happened when a train carrying two companies of the 7th Battalion, Royal Scots smashed into a local goods train that had accidentally been left on the main line; both trains were then hit by the London Euston express and all were consumed by fire. Fewer than 60 soldiers out of the original contingent of 500 were able to attend the following day's roll call.

The disastrous conduct of the war on all fronts in which the British were engaged forced the Liberal Prime Minister, Hubert Henry Asquith, to form a coalition government with the Conservatives. In one of those supreme ironies occasionally offered up by history, the Conservatives named as their price for agreeing to join the government the removal of the First Lord of the Admiralty, Winston Churchill.[1] Churchill was duly demoted to the post of Chancellor of the Duchy of Lancaster, despite his wife Clementine's plea to Asquith: 'Winston . . . has the supreme quality which I venture to say very few of your present or future cabinet possess – the power, the imagination, the deadliness to fight Germany.' She was, of course, proven to be only too right a quarter of a century later. Asquith himself clung on to power until he was replaced as Prime Minister by David Lloyd George in December 1916. Despite some successes in the middle of November at Gallipoli, Churchill nevertheless resigned his position as First Lord of the Admiralty and rejoined his regiment in France, assuming the rank of colonel commanding the 6th Battalion, Royal Scots Fusiliers.

*Mounting War Dead*
In October Bulgaria, thus far neutral, stirred from its fence-sitting and joined the Central Powers, opening up a new killing-ground with its attack on Serbia; Britain, France and Italy duly declared war. Generally speaking, however, the latter part of 1915 saw no gains or losses of any strategic note; it was a nondescript period of the war as far as the strategists were concerned. The same could not be said for the mothers, fathers, wives, sweethearts and children who were mourning the 1.6 million men who had died in the fighting by the end of the first full year of the war.

**The 'Dandy Ninth' in 1915**
For a definitive history of the Royal Scots in the Great War, we recommend Major John Ewing's *The Royal Scots 1914–1919*. The Royal Scots ('The Royal Regiment') is the oldest regiment in the British Army, having been raised in 1633 under Charles I's royal warrant. The first battle honour awarded to the regiment was Tangier 1680, and since that time it has been involved in almost every campaign the British Army has fought.

At the time of the Great War the 9th Battalion, Royal Scots, originally a volunteer corps formed by exiled Highlanders, was one of seven Scottish territorial battalions and one of four with headquarters in Edinburgh. Together with the 4th, 5th and 6th Battalions, it formed the Lothian Brigade. In this book we have used the forms '9th Royal Scots' and 'the Ninth' interchangeably.

The Ninth, as with all battalions, comprised four companies – A, B (of which Beatson was a member), C and D, each with nominally 200 men; each company had four platoons. Following the enthusiastic response to Kitchener's call for volunteers, by early November 1914 some 993 officers and men had enlisted for 'Imperial Service' with the battalion. Indeed, the Ninth was the first territorial battalion, along with the Fifth, to reach combat strength. It was – and still is – a source of pride that several of Scotland's most celebrated rugby players, former pupils of George Watson's College, joined the battalion.

In November 1914 the Ninth received orders to join the British Expeditionary Force, but as the battalion could not be spared from coastal defence duties these orders were subsequently cancelled. This gained it the nickname the 'always-never-going battalion'. In fact, under the command of Lieutenant Colonel A.S. Blair, in late February 1915 the Ninth was the first Edinburgh territorial battalion to go to the Western Front.

The battalion was popularly known as the 'Dandy Ninth' as it was the regiment's only kilted unit. This nickname was a matter of great pride and any criticism of it was taken as an insult to its honour. As Colonel Blair remarked in a letter to the *Scotsman*:

> I see in one of the Edinburgh evening papers an article . . . in which it is stated that 'one or two of the officers at the head of the Second Battalion object to the title "Dandy Ninth", and wish it dropped.' Will you kindly let it be known publicly that none of the officers and men of the real Dandy Ninth object to it in the least; in fact, we are proud of it and try to live up to it. We are the real 9th Royal Scots, and no others have any right to speak for us, or indeed to have any say in the matter, until they come out here and do their share like men. Many of them, I know, would gladly come out to help us if they could.

*Apropos* of the nickname, you will be amused to hear that the other day, I had a letter delivered to me in Flanders addressed 'The Colonel of the Dandy Ninth, France'. It had been delivered first to the Colonel of the 9th Lancers, who are also out here. He sent it to me with the following delightful letter:– 'Dear Colonel, – We never aspired to such a noble title, and so I think it must be for you. – I am, yours sincerely, etc.'[2]

At a reception held in the United Free Church Assembly Hall in Edinburgh on 15 February, a week before the battalion's departure, Lord Rosebery wished the men 'a hearty God-speed', saying:

We know the stuff of which they are made, and the stock from whence they come, and are confident that they will distinguish themselves, and bear the name of old Scotland with glory. May I be there to see when Edinburgh welcomes them home, crowned with laurels and victory.[3]

A succession of clergymen also made rousing speeches. The Revd Dr Fisher referred to 'the noble record of the Royal Scots':

They fought in America, they fought in Germany, they fought in France; they were led by the great Marlborough in his campaign in Flanders, they were led by the Great Duke of Quatre Bras and Waterloo; they fought in the Indian Mutiny, they fought in the Crimea . . . Be a good soldier of Jesus Christ.[4]

Fisher was followed by the Revd Bishop Walpole:

I doubt if ever men have gone from the shores of Britain on a greater or nobler mission than those who go to France today. They go to deliver Europe from the cruel hand . . . [of] 'blood and iron' and . . . to liberate those small nations, such as Belgium and Serbia.

I do not know any other two words which express so much meaning as the words 'Royal Scots'. I am sure that wherever the Royal Scots are, one not only finds the best fighting qualities, but that chivalry, that knighthood which, after all, is what people remember more than the courage and strength with which a man wields his weapons.[5]

And to emphasise the religious ideals with which the war had been imbued, an element that echoes through the ages, the Revd Dr Kelman added: 'This is not a fight merely of Britain against Germany, but of love against hate, of Christ against anti-Christ . . . Gentlemen, you are carrying across the ocean a splendid banner. Carry it splendidly.[6]

A week later the men of the 'Dandy Ninth' were on the move, as an anonymous private of B Company recalled:

In the very early hours . . . we heard the far-off notes of a bugle. 'Why on earth are they playing réveillé in the middle of the night?' was our thought – and we slept again. 'Wake up, everyone, it's five o'clock, the battalion leaves tonight.' Thus an excited voice from the darkness. But the Ninth, even in its sleep, was sick of rumours. . . . Some minutes later a much incensed corporal of the guard handed, in silence and injured dignity, a typed sheet to our sergeant in the corner; the magic words were read out again, and we awoke.

Of the orgy of scrubbing, the locked gates, the tense excitement, the final kit inspection, nothing need be said. Somehow the news spread, and in the grey of the winter's afternoon relatives and friends began to gather in little groups first outside and then in. As night came on and seven drew near, the excitement deepened, till the bugle came to our relief – 'The Campbells are coming, hurra, hurra. Fall in! Fall in!'

That last scene will never fade. Snowy streets and the dark night, the men lining across the street, sergeants flitting about, the officers standing quietly, everything subdued. Then the roll-call in whispered, quivering voices – the last! – and a moment's 'at ease'. 'All present, sir,' says the Sergeant-Major quietly, a hush, and the well-known deep voice (a shade deeper perhaps) of the Captain in the well-known words but fraught with how much meaning! 'B Company. 'Shun! Slope arms, advance in fours from the right', and our own officer's sharper voice '7 Platoon, form fours, right, by the left, left wheel, quick march!'

We entrained quietly in Princes Street Station about eight, gave the first detachment a cheer as they steamed out, and left ourselves at nine, just after the third and last detachment marched in with two bands and great cheering.[7]

The following day the Ninth boarded the requisitioned cargo ship HMT *Inventor* at Southampton: 'Going aboard was as quiet as entraining – a few staff-officers, no spectators. It seemed as though we were in another world, shut off from friends and the civil population, set apart for a great task.'[8] It was during this Channel crossing that Beatson started to write his diary.

Like many soldiers on the front line, the men of the 'Dandy Ninth' were avid letter writers and diary keepers, partly to relieve an often tedious and mundane existence, but also to stay in touch with family and friends seeking contact with their loved ones. One striking theme in the letters is the constant demand for food parcels. Beatson himself wrote almost daily to both Carrie and his sister Bella, as well as to various other people, his mother having died before the war. We are fortunate that a number of his comrades' letters and diary entries were published during the war years; they attest to the courage, resilience, intelligence and humanity of members of the Ninth. In particular, during the years 1914 and 1915 Scottish regional newspapers such as the *Scotsman* and *Edinburgh Evening News* were full of vivid accounts of life in the trenches, albeit these were heavily censored and biased. In these early months of the war the Royal Scots' accounts of their adventures on all fronts, not just in France and Belgium, were a regular feature. Sadly, as the war dragged on into 1916 such testimonies became less frequent, and ceased to be published, column inches instead being taken up by ever-lengthening reports of casualties and official 'rolls of honour' listing those 'who have died for their country'.

Another contemporary account upon which the editors of this book have drawn is *9th Royal Scots (T.F.) B Company on Active*

*Service, From a Private's Diary, February–May 1915*, which was published in Edinburgh in 1916 with proceeds donated to a fund for 'Ninth' men disabled in the war.

Most of the published accounts, once passed by the Press Censor, were reproduced anonymously. It is pure speculation, of course, but the similarity of phrases contained in some of these reports and in Beatson's diary suggests the intriguing possibility that Beatson himself was the author of some of them.

A number of themes recur throughout the accounts of Beatson and his comrades, including a sense of admiration for all soldiers from the furthest corners of the British Empire; mixed feelings about the French army; and respect for the opposing German soldiers. Respect is also forthcoming for the British generals in command, tinged with a growing exasperation with political life back in Britain; and, all the hardships notwithstanding, delight at their 'great adventure'.

The Ninth fought alongside the Canadians and were second to none in their admiration for the colonial soldiers. Beatson wrote: 'Getting ready to go into the trenches; the "Princess Pats"[9] are a game lot. Went into battle last night with cigs between their teeth.' Another member of the Ninth, writing from his hospital bed after being wounded in the initial fighting at the Second Battle of Ypres, recalled:

I was advancing along with the rest when a shell burst and buried another chap and myself, and the fumes from it knocked me out. I thought it was all up. I came round all right, and discovered I had not got a scratch. I could see men lying all over the field, and the rifle and shell-fire was still going strong. I started to crawl away when a bullet hit me in the left leg – so that settled it. I stopped where I was until I was picked up. I got lifted by the Canadians, and they took me to a dressing station and fixed me up. It is only a very slight wound I have got, and it will be all right in a day or two. I was taken in the train down to another Canadian hospital in Boulogne, and it is simply heaven. The Canadians are splendid people; they can't do enough for you.[10]

It was not only the Canadians who were admired. During the Second Battle of Ypres a private in B Company wrote:

> In the afternoon we saw a great sight – the Lahore Division advancing into action. They came through the wood in endless files, stripped off their coats and packs at the edge, and in open order went across the shell-torn field to the St Jean road and the ground we had left. With shells crashing all about them, they went steadily on as if on manoeuvres, and when they disappeared from sight we breathed a wish for their success. Those little, dark figures, impassive and cool, stirred our sympathy as nothing else. Not the Islands only, but the Empire, were battling here.[11]

Relations with individual French soldiers were generally friendly, but feelings towards the French army as a whole were rather more ambivalent. Here is Beatson writing on 30 March:

> French soldiers are resting and very interesting to talk to although laborious. Good-hearted fellows . . . We always tinkle our glasses to 'La Belle Alliance' and leave each other with a handshake and a salaam. Only one drawback to their character is their inbred viciousness.

And on 27 September: 'Battalions of French infantry passed us on their way back last Tuesday. The men were of a standard higher than the usual of the French but the march discipline was atrocious. Even with the trumpets blaring and bands playing, they shuffled along any old way.'

Likewise, relationships with individual French and Belgian families, whose resilience Beatson admired, were warmer than with the community at large. Beatson wrote:

> It is no small thing to enjoy the friendship of the home circle of Chez Lepan for even three weeks. They reveal a much more wholesome side of the French character than is usually presented.

James Beatson (right) with his mother Elizabeth, brother Donald and sister Isabella; in all James had eight brothers and sisters.

Beatson's father John, in Royal Scots Pipe-Major's uniform.

Private James Nicol
Beatson, No. 2024, 9th
Royal Scots, probably
taken in August 1914,
aged 22.

'Left Edinburgh two
nights ago, the less I say
of how I felt the better. I
purpose [intend] keeping
a rough record of the
future days so that when
I return, (may God grant
it), I may the more
faithfully recount them to
you.'
The first daily entry in
Beatson's diary.

2

Thursday 25th. Feb.
1915

Left Edin. two nights ago the less
I say of how I felt the better. I Purpose
keeping a rough record of future days
so that when I return. (May God grant it)
I may the more faithfully recount them
to you. We have been on the water since
four o'clock yesterday afternoon and are
only some half-mile of shore. The train
journey was very comfortable but since
coming on board the Kaiser has something
to answer for. lack of space and the
cold made sleeping impossible. While the
continual clattering of hob-nailed boots
on the iron-plating was an in        nable
barrier to those who got ove
Two Lascars wandered about
early, selling us tea at 2 a cup

'We know the stuff of which they are made, and the stock from whence they come, and are confident that they will distinguish themselves, and bear the name of old Scotland with glory.' (Lord Rosebery). Officers of the 9th Royal Scots pictured at a training camp before the War in 1914.

'Weeks of disappointment, rumours galore, kit inspections, and, worst of all, false farewells had made us bitter . . . the always-never-going-battalion.' (Anonymous Private in B Company). 9th Royal Scots resting during training exercises at Leith, 1914.

**'The boat was used before the outbreak of war as a cattle transport . . . and the cattle have left a few keepsakes – worse luck!'** The 9th Royal Scots aboard the requisitioned cargo ship HMT *Inventor* en route to France on 24 February 1915.

**'We had furries served out here . . . We came across in a cattle boat, were fed on cattle biscuits, wore cattle coats.'** Argyll and Sutherland Highlanders wearing their government issue fur jackets ('furries') usually made from goat or sheepskin, 1915.

**'I'm certain that Dickebusch is full of pro-Germans and that they give away information as the price of their safety.'** Dickebusch as Beatson would have known it, 1915.

**'We were relieved last night, dragged ourselves for eight miles to the little wooden hut at Vlamertinghe.'** The Belgian village of Vlamertinghe after heavy shelling.

**'A party of us went digging trenches today.'** 2nd Royal Scots Fusiliers digging trenches north of the Menin Road, October 1914.

**'The roads are lined with . . . tall trees.'** Dispatch riders on a typical tree-lined road near Dickebusch, 1914.

'The streets are lined with the kind of building that is met throughout France . . . "cafés" with seats in front.' An old French lady serving coffee to British troops relaxing near Armentières, in 1916.

'Nobody could be anything else but happy.' 51st Highlanders.

'A letter to Carrie and a note to her Dad ran me into nine pages, which relieved my mind a great deal.'

'The blankets haven't been given us, so we retire thusly – socks on, kilt loosened, jacket buttoned only at the waist, greatcoat turned upside down and legs slid into the sleeves. This leaves you to curl up and chew the mud off the foot of the coat.'

The types of the villagers are: the men, gaunt, grey-haired with straggling moustache, dirty shirt sleeves, slack pants and red waistband, a sort of broken-down brigand; the women, heavy, clumsy, agricultural, and nearly all in the way of increasing the family. We have to try and forget their dirt and live down their suspicions for the sake of the Entente Cordiale. . . . Everybody is to be treated with cold distrust for the sake of the Entente Cordiale. I remember how Zola . . . despised this breed of humanity peculiar to agricultural France.

While his hatred of Kaiser Wilhelm for his role in instigating the war was consistent and unremitting – 'Damn the Kaiser and curse his breed forever' – Beatson, in common with the average 'Tommy', had a grudging respect for the Germans he was fighting.

The Germans opposite us are to be respected as fighters . . . Our procedure and trenches were childish in comparison . . . We British are game to the last, but damned stupid at times, and this was one such time last weekend. . . . It's only too true that we're fighting at present with kid gloves on, while the Huns are going at it tooth and nail.

Naturally, as the casualties began to mount, opinions hardened; here is Beatson writing a week after the end of the Second Battle of Ypres: 'Nobody could be anything else but happy – the destruction of the Huns would complete it.' Nevertheless, it seems that Beatson would readily have fraternised, at least to some extent, with the enemy had it not been for General French's directive prohibiting such behaviour following the famous 1914 Christmas 'truce': 'A German shouted across, "How do you like your job tonight, Jock"? Unfortunately we have had orders to cut them dead when they become familiar.'

Interestingly, there are noticeable differences in how Beatson and his fellow soldiers viewed the constituent 'nationalities' within the German army. Of the four kingdoms that formed the unified Germany in 1871, the Prussians were the most militaristic and were despised as arrogant bullies:

The German soldiers are heartily tired but the officers hold
their heads high and freely brandish their revolvers at the
slightest evidence of irritation at the cast-iron discipline. This
is the sort of thing that is going to help us when we've knocked
the feet from the Prussian bully-caste.

In comparison, the Bavarians and Saxons were considered quite mild.
A week after being injured at the Second Battle of Ypres, Private
Charles Henderson of the 9th Royal Scots told a correspondent from
the *Edinburgh Evening News*: '[The Bavarians] don't appear to bother
themselves much about the war . . . It would have been a very different
kind of war had all the enemy been like them.'[12] Indeed, it was along
sections of the front line manned by soldiers from Bavaria and Saxony
that the 1914 Christmas truce had broken out.

Beatson often alludes to the front-line soldier's exasperation with
certain aspects of life back home: 'curse the incompetency of
pothouse lawyers'. On 29 April he wrote:

If some of the men in the homeland could see and feel, their
heads would come off their chests and their hands off their
bellies . . . Our artillery seemed miserably inadequate. I only
wish the fellows who grumble at home over a few coppers or
hours overtime were sent out here; they would understand
things a bit better from our point of view.

One of Beatson's comrades in B Company noted bitterly:

Men were 'striking' at home at this time for war-bonuses and
more pay. We wondered how they would have liked our
experience: constant work or marching, day and night, for three
days, no sleep, little food, and less to drink, and precious little
pay at the end – if ever we got it![13]

This sentiment is mirrored in a letter from another soldier with the
9th Royal Scots that was published in the *Scotsman* on 2 June:

The soldiers out here feel confident that when the time comes
the great advance can be made. The public at home do not seem

so confident. Everybody who is doing anything at all seems to be getting criticised by those who are doing nothing. It makes us sick to see French and Kitchener and Churchill criticised by a lot of armchair strategists.[14]

These passages highlight an important aspect of the war in 1915: the widening gulf between those at the front and those at home. The divide was wide enough already, not least because the unique experiences of the front-line soldier formed an inescapable rite of passage that left him unable to equate his life with those who had not been so initiated. The experience was, per se, so remarkable that those who had not endured it could neither share in it nor understand it. Consequently, soldiers of this war, indeed of most wars, are renowned for their reticence in sharing their experiences. It did not help that the supply of shells to the British artillery was indeed 'miserably inadequate', certainly in comparison to the mountainous stocks of all types of shells held by the Germans and 'shared' daily with the Allies. The consequent demands on British industry to increase supply resulted in workers striking for more pay. Beatson's remarks, in particular, illustrate precisely the anger felt on the front line at this affront to the bravery of the soldiers, most of whom at this stage were volunteers.

On a more positive note, soldiers on the front line gratefully received parcels of food and other 'luxuries' as well as letters and magazines; here is Beatson again: 'What a deluge of cake, chocolate and the hundred other things that go to make parcels.' Certainly efforts to provide for Scottish regiments were highly organised. In Edinburgh a 'Blanket Committee' was established, and its Convener reported in November 1914:

> More blankets have come to us from all quarters of Scotland – from Oban in the West to St Andrews in the East, and from Aberdeenshire and Banffshire in the North to the Border towns, in addition to those from Edinburgh and district . . . One beautiful Angora shawl . . . is of historic interest, having been

worn during the Crimean and Franco-Prussian Wars . . . Four hundred blankets have been gifted to the 7th Royal Scots and 500 to the 9th Royal Scots.[15]

The Scottish National Flag Day held on 28 November 1914 raised some £7,000. The report of the sub-committee appointed to expend the funds detailed the 'comforts [provided] for Scottish soldiers in the field'.[16] In addition to hundreds of special requests for watches, shaving outfits, etc., the list comprised:

| | £ | s | d |
|---|---|---|---|
| Mechanical lighters (including matches) | 200 | 0 | 0 |
| Bagpipes, gramophones, melodeons and other musical instruments | 200 | 0 | 0 |
| Currant loaf and shortbread | 1,432 | 13 | 4 |
| Dried fruit | 319 | 7 | 0 |
| Woollen garments and comforts | 597 | 18 | 2 |
| General comforts, including tobacco, pipes, pencils, etc | 100 | 0 | 0 |
| Condensed milk | 298 | 1 | 6 |
| Sweets and chocolate | 355 | 15 | 3 |
| Necessities for prisoners in Germany | 75 | 0 | 0 |
| Candles | 15 | 12 | 6 |
| Magic lanterns and slides | 200 | 0 | 0 |
| Literature | 250 | 0 | 0 |
| Cocoa and milk | 134 | 7 | 5 |
| General comforts | 454 | 14 | 10 |
| Towels | 450 | 5 | 2 |
| Writing pads, containing notepaper, envelopes, postcards, etc | 324 | 2 | 0 |
| Socks | 76 | 3 | 10 |
| Liquorice pellets | 10 | 0 | 0 |
| Field glasses | 24 | 0 | 0 |

Many letters and postcards expressing the soldiers' appreciation were received by the organisers, including this from a private in the Ninth:

> I received your parcel of chocolate as long ago as the 4th of April, and although I have been so long in acknowledging it, I can assure you that I am very grateful for your kindness. The chocolate was excellent, as others also can testify, and it arrived undamaged . . . We are . . . enjoying life generally. Our mails and parcels reach us here, so nothing else matters.[17]

Finally, the soldiers' delight at their adventure remained surprisingly undiminished despite the privations of life in the trenches:

> There are compensations. There shines out above everything, like a star in the expanse of night, the glamour and romance of being an actor in the greatest drama of the world's history. No matter how hard a thing it is to endure, no matter how utterly miserable, no matter how dangerous and cruel, it is something we wouldn't miss for worlds.[18]

On their arrival in France the men of the Ninth were immediately sent 'up the line' and attached to the 81st Brigade, part of the 27th Division. The 81st Brigade was headquartered north of the Menin Road at Hooge in Belgium, and comprised two other units, the 1st Battalion, Argyll & Sutherland Highlanders and the 1st Battalion, Royal Scots.

On 9 March 1915 Colonel Blair, briefly detained in hospital suffering from bronchitis and influenza, wrote:

> The Ninth have done everything asked of them up to now splendidly, and have been much praised for their smartness, embarking, disembarking, entraining, marching, etc. We had a week's continuous travelling at one time, being twenty-six hours in the train, chiefly in cattle trucks, and then long marches of from twelve to fifteen miles. At the end it was a miserable billet in barns and the like, but not a complaint or a grumble.
>
> One company has gone up to the trenches this week for instruction. Another follows afterwards, until all have been

instructed sufficiently to stand on their own legs. So far the men's health has been good, notwithstanding the terrible weather and the appalling state of the roads. There has been only one casualty, as yet, when a young lad accidentally shot his foot cleaning his rifle. It was not serious, I am glad to say.[19]

It was not long, however, before the Ninth suffered their first casualties in battle. On 14 March, just two weeks into active service, Sergeant Thomas Chrichton was killed and three others wounded as C Company held the front line against a German attack near St Eloi. Although the stark realities of war were becoming all too apparent, the spirit of the men remained unflinchingly high; Colonel Blair again, writing on 24 March:

> We are still going strong, and the men are extraordinarily keen and ready to take up any job that comes their way, however hard or dangerous. It is really wonderful how these town-bred lads, accustomed to every comfort at home, have settled down to this awfully hard life – always cheerful and smiling. Anyone who does venture a 'grouse' gets sat on at once by his comrades. I wish you could see the Battalion as they are at present. They would create a sensation marching down Princes Street – every man plastered with mud from head to foot carrying a heavy pack and a great heavy coat as well, but every one of the boys with his face clean, well shaved, and a proud determined look in his eyes that he means to see this thing through.
>
> There is nothing of the 'Dandy' now in his personal appearance, but there is in his spirit, and he is clean white through and through.[20]

In a letter to his parents, published in the *Edinburgh Evening News*, a private in the Ninth picked up the same theme, as he described passing 'from a dream into life':

> To the left stood the mere framework of a little village street, and a cat, driven crazy by desolation and hunger, wailed pitifully somewhere among the ruins. All was still save for the

distant roll of a gun or the occasional crack of a rifle. It seemed to be as though even the Angel of Death must be afraid of the spot and would not venture near it, till the memory of a certain letter from home sprang before me and the scene was instantly changed, for I saw the Angel of Life and Victory hovering over the lonely pile, and I was comforted.

And when we are back, and the candle is flickering from the log in the tent and we sit opposite each other smoking and thinking of the old folk, there is after all but one opinion, that none of us would have it otherwise, that none of us are sorry to have left peace and safety and embraced instead discomfort and danger and suffering.

We are the 'Dandy' Ninth no longer; we have passed beyond that into something more solid and cruel, yet withal into something more manly; we have passed as it were from a dream into life; and often here in the wood you may see men look into each other's eyes and say in the same breath: 'This is the life, brother.' Strange that it should be so, but it is true.[21]

On 7 April D Company suffered more than 50 casualties when their billet at a convent in Ypres was shelled. The following day Colonel Blair wrote to the relatives of each of the men who had been killed; here is his letter to a man who lost his only son:

Dear Mr Mackenzie

I deeply regret to send you the sad news of the death of your son, Private C.A. Mackenzie, No. 2208, yesterday morning by the bursting of a shell in D Company's billets. The poor lad was killed outright with six others, and a considerable number wounded – some seriously. The Germans started shelling the place about 7 a.m., and several fell right in the men's billets while they were sleeping after a hard night's work digging in the trenches. We are all deeply distressed at this heavy blow, and our warmest sympathy goes out to you in the great loss you have sustained.

Your poor boy was buried yesterday alongside his comrades

by the Scottish Presbyterian Chaplain here . . . in the presence
of all the officers and men available, and a cross will be at once
erected marking the exact spot. I have no further particulars at
present, as the rest of the battalion are some miles away at the
immediate front, and write under difficulties underground, and
with shells and bullets flying overhead.

I would like, however, to tell you how proud we are of your
boy's work and of his courage and devotion to his old corps, and
I sincerely hope you will be given strength to bear the heavy
blow which has fallen on you. With deepest sympathy.

I am,

Yours very sincerely,

A.S. Blair,

Lt–Col., Commanding 9th Royal Scots[22]

The 27th Division (to which the Ninth was attached) was responsible
for a section of trenches 4 miles due east of Ypres. The relief
arrangements put in place by the 81st Brigade meant that one
battalion remained in rest while the other two garrisoned the front
line, a fourth battalion being stationed at regimental barracks. Just
prior to the German attack on 22 April the men of the 9th Royal Scots
were quartered in huts at Vlamertinghe, due west of Ypres, expecting
four days' rest.

### The Second Battle of Ypres

The Second Battle of Ypres lasted five weeks and was arguably one of
the pivotal battles of 1915, indeed of the entire war on the Western
Front. If the Germans had broken through following their chlorine
gas attack on the Gravenstafel Ridge, they would have cut off the
Allied soldiers left exposed in the Ypres salient, captured Ypres itself
and probably succeeded in pushing the BEF back to and then across
the English Channel (certainly this was the preferred option at home
should the British be cut off from the French). Only a few months
into the war, Ypres had become the symbol of Allied resistance to

Germany's aggression, and so it was to remain throughout the conflict.

The 9th Royal Scots played a crucial role in supporting the heroic defence of St Julien by the 2nd Brigade of the Canadian Expeditionary Force (CEF). The Canadians suffered grievous losses in defending the line: three-quarters of the 800-strong 10th Battalion CEF were killed or wounded on the first day of fighting. During the course of the battle, over 300 soldiers of the Ninth were killed, wounded, listed as missing or taken prisoner. Beatson's account, written a week after the fighting commenced, records: 'I saw the wounded on all sides. I did what little I could but it is heart-rending to hear the fellows asking for help and see the dead lying so very still.' The fighting started on the evening of 22 April, having been preceded by a heavy German bombardment of Ypres:

> All day long they had been shelling a town in our lines. An Argyll said that their gigantic shells were like 'engineers' shops' being pitched about, and the town was soon in flames and ruins. Following upon the severe shelling, the Germans – reinforced, it was said, by Hindenburg and 500,000 men – advanced, and the French were sorely pressed. We were ordered up in support. What a sight it was! Roads and railways were congested with troops being rushed towards the enemy. Shell fire or no shell fire, we had to get there, and our passage through the blazing town, with shells exploding on all sides and shrapnel falling like rain, was an experience never to be forgotten. I hope we may have nothing like it again.[23]

Private Charles Henderson of the Ninth recalled:

> We had come out of the trenches after a spell of four days, and were resting, when the cry arose that German aeroplanes were hovering over our lines. We could see them flying at a great height and dropping star lights to guide the fire of the German guns. At that moment the Canadians, who were resting near us, were ordered up to relieve the French, but before they got to the

trenches they met some of the French coming back, shouting, 'The Allemands have broken through'. They (the French) seemed to be pretty badly scared, as if something unusual had happened. Then we got word to turn out, and marched ahead to support them.[24]

Another of Beatson's comrades described soldiers returning from the nearby village 'with the extraordinary story of Frenchmen running down the roads from the front with fear in their faces and tales of retreat. Also of a strange acrid taste in the air. We quietly began to prepare.'[25] He also described what the Ninth witnessed as they approached Ypres:

The main road was a sight we shall never forget. It was absolutely solid with troops, marching, marching, marching – to Ypres. Fugitives were there too, transport wagons were at the side or parked to let the infantry pass. Down the side roads where we went gun limbers were rattling along. The turmoil was indescribable. Something *had* happened for sure.

The sight was tragic. . . . It was very dark but Ypres was lit up by a solid mass of flame. As we looked, fascinated and horrified, we could see the dark mass of the Cathedral and Cloth Hall backed by the wall of flame, whose crackling we could hear above the stillness. The flames were leaping high, so high that the Cathedral's square tower and the Cloth Hall's delicate pinnacles were picked out and silhouetted in the night sky. The story of the pathetic fugitives by road and railway was clear to us now, and as we lay on the ground, chilled, we talked in whispers of the horror of the sight from which our eyes could not turn. Ypres of happy memory – in flames![26]

At midnight the Royal Scots' immediate task was to make their way through Ypres itself:

We had to run the gauntlet through the burning shelled town. We went, platoon by platoon, at one hundred yards' interval, hugging the walls of the dark side of the square, at the double, past the blazing quarter by the canal, with the hot breath of the flames on our cheeks, and out to the Menin road beyond. It was a last terrific sight.[27]

And then they had to find shelter:

Once through the town we were comparatively safe till we attempted to cross the fields, where we encountered another storm of 'coal boxes'. When these fell, they threw up spouts of earth and stones 30 feet high, and how we escaped is a mystery. How we raced forward! Dodging round a farmhouse we lay in a field till afternoon. The shells continued to fall, but they were half a field away, and we sat tight. About two o'clock we were ordered to resume the advance, and did so along the front of two big guns. The shells, seeking the guns, came sailing over us again, and we opened out in skirmishing order. We were soon spotted, and instead of getting shells intended for the guns, we got a consignment all for ourselves. A shell landed in our right hand platoon! I closed my eyes in horror, but when I looked again the smoke had lifted and the men were sorting themselves out. Miraculous, as it appeared, no one was seriously hurt!

Across two fields we advanced at an easy pace, and as we breasted a rise a terrific hail of bullets met us from four machine-guns. I can tell you we flopped down in double quick time. To remain there, however, was to court death, and the order came for a rapid advance. With the support of gun or side fire we doubled across the open ground against no one knew what odds! When we reached the hedge at the far side of the field we thought for the moment that we were safe, and we lay down for a 'breather'. Immediately the air was rent with cries and moans, and we realised, too late, that the hedge was a 'mark'. Men were hit on all sides. Another man and I bandaged Sergt Mackay's wound, and managed to get him into a ditch, where we lay for half-an-hour. Mr Lyon shouted at length, 'We can't lie here. Come on! I'll go first.' Before one could respond he forced a way through the hedge, and lay down waiting for us. We followed immediately, and after a burst of rapid fire on the enemy we pushed on across another field under heavier fire than ever.

Half-way across we halted and lay down. I was hit on the head with the earth thrown up by a bullet which hit the ground some inches away. Forward again we pressed, leaving a wake of stricken men. Reaching another hedge we collapsed in a ditch, and then, most unaccountably, the firing ceased. We opened fire on the farmhouse ahead, but elicited no response. Rushing on, we sought shelter on the outskirts of the farm, where we remained for over an hour, while patrols were despatched to investigate. So absolutely dead beat were some of us that we fell sound asleep! On the return of the patrols, we vacated our position and went to the left, past the remains of other troops. By this time it was night, and the scene as disclosed in the moonlight was wonderfully impressive. The ground was strewn with rifles and equipment, and here and there the moonlight glinted on a bayonet. On all hands lay the dead and wounded.[28]

By three o'clock in the morning the men of the Ninth were ensconced in dug-outs in Potijze Wood, a mile or so east of Ypres, where they awaited their orders. The situation was naturally very confused and the following account benefits from hindsight after the event:

The French holding the line to the north of Ypres had retreated, unprepared and terror-stricken before the first attack of the new enemy – Gas, in volumes so great that the air had been tainted even at Vlamertinghe, miles away. A great gap had thus been made in the line, through which enemy troops were pouring, almost surrounding the left of the Canadians, which, attacked in front and flank, was being bent back on the village of St Julien, six or seven miles or so north-east of Ypres. To meet this, every available battalion for miles around (the Ninth among the number) was being thrown into the gap to hold the line and help the Canadians, who were heroically holding on.[29]

Gas was an ever-present danger:

> The Germans brought their guns to bear on us again, and soon 'Jack Johnsons' and other shells emitting poisonous gases were dropping on us. The gas appeared to be a vapour of a yellowish colour as it floated in the sunshine. It made our eyes burn and dried up our throats so that we could hardly speak. Fortunately there was a fairly strong wind blowing, and the gases were carried away before anyone was overcome, though several of our men complained of the effects. Had it not been for the wind, we would probably have suffered severely from the fumes.[30]

At ten o'clock on the morning of 23 April the Ninth received the order to move on. The original intention was for the whole battalion to advance on the German line as part of a hastily assembled Composite Brigade formed with the Duke of Cornwall's Light Infantry (DCLI). However, at half past midday, on reaching the village of Wieltje, Colonel Blair received urgent orders from the brigadier to take two companies to St Julien to support the Canadians. A Company made its way through Wieltje safely, but B Company suffered severely under enemy fire, with 18 men wounded:

> It was a rather shaken [B] company which gathered itself for the next advance.
>
> This time we were wiser, dividing into sections and going by the fields, with every possible cover taken advantage of. And we got to within a few hundred yards of St Julien, a little group of houses over and among which shells were every moment bursting. On the way, in the farm-steadings we had sheltered in, we came on Canadians, just one or two, whose story of the night before was terrific.
>
> Since then we have often wondered why we were not all wiped out at St Julien that day![31]

At quarter past three in the afternoon C and D Companies were ordered to attack with the DCLI and the York and Lancaster Regiment. An hour later A and B Companies received an urgent

message from the Commanding Officer of the Composite Brigade to
return at once to support the attack on the German line at St Jean.

> We had a hard time of it. The Germans were using some sort of
> gas, and as it burst it made you sick and about choked you. Our
> boys advanced right up to the Germans under a very heavy fire.
> They were falling along the whole line, and we could not do
> anything for them at the time. We managed to get the Germans
> on the run, but it took a bit of doing. They outnumbered us
> about ten to one as far as I could make out.[32]
>
> It appears that the Germans inferred from our steady
> advance across the fields that we were the advance guard of a
> tremendous force, and they actually vacated the hill which they
> held! Sounds a bit thick, but it is said to be true.[33]

For the next three days the Ninth held the line north of St Jean.

> Shells were frequent and directed against a Canadian battery of
> three guns firing away pluckily a little to our right.
>
> Whether we were the front line or not we never knew, but we
> supposed we were, for there was great activity behind us.
>
> We knew now that the line had been broken; we could see the
> patch of wood where through a dreadful night and day the
> Canadians had faced unnumbered foes; we knew that British
> reinforcements must be hurling themselves into that hell of
> shell and machine-gun fire.
>
> We looked on – but in terrific anxiety, more for our unknown
> comrades than ourselves; yet we too expected any moment the
> order to advance . . . and take our share, few though we were. It
> was perhaps the longest day most of us ever lived through.[34]

On 27 April the Ninth was relieved by the West Kent Regiment and
proceeded to Potijze Wood and later to Sanctuary Wood: 'All
afternoon troops in thousands filed through the wood, and we
watched fascinated. We knew, too, that our job was done. We were no
longer needed "in support of the Canadians".'[35] The battle continued
until 24 May; Beatson wrote: 'We waited all [day] in a state of tension,

we could smell the gas and the wind was blowing strongly against us.
. . . We, however, it seemed had re-established all lost ground with
some additional trenches.' And the following day he wrote: 'The crisis
appeared to be over and . . . a column of buses drew up and we had a
welcome drive back.'

On 26 May the men of the Ninth were visited by Major-General
Snow, commanding the 27th Division:

> [We] heard from him that the Division had earned a good rest,
> and was to be shifted to another 'more healthy' part of the line.
> And in the early morning of the 28th the battalion marched
> off, leaving Ypres and its memories, forth to new ventures and
> fresh service.[36]

The Ninth now headed south to trenches near Armentières, an
altogether quieter proposition than the Ypres salient; on 18 June
Colonel Blair wrote:

> We had our clothes on for six weeks without a change, and doing
> very dirty work all the time, but as soon as we came out of the
> trenches we got hot baths and a good scrub.
> It was different up there, as there were no baths, and if there
> were we couldn't have used them. Here it is a very different story
> – clean trenches, wide and safe – very little danger, almost no firing,
> a charming part of France, and a good town near, with excellent
> baths for us when we come out. At present we want nothing in
> particular, so far as I can see. We have had a glorious rest since the
> battle of Ypres, and though back in the trenches here, some miles
> south of our former line, are as happy and merry as sand-boys.[37]

In November the rest of the 27th Division moved to Salonika[38] to
prepare for an assault on Bulgaria. The Ninth, however, remained in
France, initially with the 5th Division and then with the Third Army
reserve. In March 1916 it was transferred to the 51st (Highland)
Division with which it served for the next two years, including, most
fatefully for James Beatson, at the Battle of the Somme.

# Prologue

At 5 o'clock on the morning of Tuesday, 23 February 1915 the men of the 9th Battalion, Royal Scots were roused from their slumber by a bugler playing reveille. Months of impatient waiting – during which the 'always-never-going battalion' had become the laughing stock of Edinburgh – were over. No more unsubstantiated rumours, endless kit inspections and false farewells to loved ones. Later that day, they would depart for the war.

That evening the 'Dandy Ninth' marched through the dark, snowy streets of Edinburgh to Princes Street station. As one of Private Beatson's comrades in B Company later wrote:

> There was no band, no wild excitement, or hysterical farewell. The key-note was a quiet note of pride, a steady facing of the Unknown, relief that we were actually off, which softened at the time the 'sadness of farewell' – all unemotional perhaps, but impressive.[39]

The battalion boarded trains in three detachments, B Company leaving the station at around 9 o'clock. The journey south was uneventful. Breakfast, consisting of a meat sandwich, Melton Mowbray pork pie and hot coffee, was taken at Crewe. Even as the men headed through the Midlands in the late winter sunshine, there were rumours that their destination was Winchester for a spell of divisional training. However, the train did not stop and steamed on to Southampton, bringing with it the sudden recognition that they were most certainly heading for France.

At around 4 o'clock in the afternoon, with the sun about to set, the 9th Royal Scots, some Coldstream Guards and elements of the Army

Service Corps embarked on HMT *Inventor*, a cargo ship requisitioned as a troop carrier. Still there was no fanfare, just sober concentration on the task ahead. 'We watched the arrival of hospital ships, and realised that that was the way not a few of us would return.'[40]

The *Inventor* laid to down the river; it did not cross the Channel until the following day, at which point Private Beatson started writing his diary.

\*   \*   \*

# Part I:

# Arrival and Life in the Trenches

## ~ *First Entry* ~

James N. Beatson No. 2024 B Company, 9th Royal Scots

In the event of my death, William Swan No. 2288 or Cecil Valentine No. 2355 or failing those, I can trust the good fellowship of any of my comrades to do me and those who love me the favour of sending this record to my father John Beatson, 22 Downfield Place, Edinburgh.

February 1915

*The 9th Royal Scots landed at Le Havre and travelled by train to the fields of Flanders and their section of the Western Front, where the opposing Allied and German armies were 'entrenched'. They joined the 81st Brigade of the British Army's 27th Division.*

## ~ *Channel Crossing* ~

English Channel
Thursday, 25th February 1915

Left Edinburgh two nights ago, the less I say of how I felt the better. I purpose [*intend*] keeping a rough record of the future days so that when I return (may God grant it), I may the more faithfully recount them to you.

We have been on the water since four o'clock yesterday

afternoon and are only some half mile off shore. The train journey was very comfortable but since coming on board the Kaiser has something to answer for. Lack of space and the cold make sleeping impossible, while the continual clattering of hobnailed boots on the iron plating was an impregnable barrier to those who got over the first.

Two Lascars [*Indian sailors*] wandered about late and early, selling vile tea at 2d a cup. In fact hawking is their main occupation; tea, oranges, biscuits at the highest prices obtainable. They are in general small and weak looking with a slight knowledge of English and hail from Calcutta. The boat was used before the outbreak of war as a cattle transport from Liverpool to Calcutta and the cattle have left a few keepsakes – worse luck!

Today the sun is bright but cold still. Dredgers, minesweepers (this line means that I got a blow from a block which some fool upset which about finished this diary and me) and small craft churn up and down. Hospital ships are anchored here and there. Last night as we sailed past them a low cheer was raised on both sides, low because strict orders were given for silence. A seaplane has whirred overhead once or twice, searching like a hawk for some submarine rat.

## ~ First Day in France ~

Le Havre
Friday, 26th February

A brilliant morning on Havre pier, the sun warming the morning air and glittering the waters.

We sailed last night on a sea as calm as a millpond, relying on our strong guards for a safe journey. All were ordered below and a night much better than the previous one was spent in sleep. We got a hurried breakfast, Bill and I, no tea, and I for one landed in France with a big hunger and some French and a few coppers to ease it. An old lady with a paralysed left hand, in charge of the 'Ligue Nationale

Antealcoolique',[41] sold buttered rolls at a penny a time. 'Chocolat', 'petite beurre', etc. were on sale but, strange enough, no wine (although its harmlessness is famous) was to be had.

A few Indians with donkey carts and Frenchmen were moving about the sheds, and as if to enforce the terms of discipline on the minds of new arrivals, squads of prisoners toiled and sweated under a bullying sergeant. I was told the principal offences are drunkenness and disobedience to officers. One carries the V.C., another is in for five years for shooting his own forefinger off.

March 1915

*The 9th Royal Scots spent most of the month digging and fortifying trenches near the Belgian village of Dickebusch, within a mile of the front line. On 14 March the battalion endured its first taste of trench warfare and suffered its first casualties in holding the front-line trenches against an attack by the Germans near St Eloi. In all, two Royal Scots were killed and fifty wounded.*

### ~ From France to Belgium ~

L'Abeele
Monday, 1st March

Arrived at Boeschepe last night over the French frontier into Belgium. But to begin where I left off.

We left Havre Pier on Friday afternoon to march some four miles to a rest camp. No attempt was made to raise a marching song. We were all eyes for anything new.

The streets are lined with the kind of building that is met throughout France, flashy and toy like. You expect to see 'Made in Germany' stamped on the back. You can see them in 'Pathe Frére Comédies' in the New Picture House any night. 'Appartements' with little balconies outside, door-windows, 'cafés' with seats in front under an awning and plants around. 'Maisons' set in rock gardens, haughty and 'insouciant' as a Boilian female* and the 'counseilleurs' have the same straining after realism as Zola or Balzac for they take no trouble to screen the urinals, or the fact that the ladies have as much right to animal comfort as the men.

The only thing that the Mademoiselles have to learn our girls is hairdressing. We have been early on the move often, but have never failed to find the girls clean-faced and elaborately coiffed. They know that nothing disturbs love like a slatternly appearance. They live to love or to inspire love and lust; there is no difference to most French women.

After climbing an abominable hill we reached camp, got settled in tents and I went to the Y.M.C.A. where I wrote you to the accompaniment of some amateur singing. The place was packed and stories from the Front were to be heard on all sides.

Reveille at 5.30 next morning, Saturday, after a pretty fair night's sleep, and off at 7.15 to the 'Foie de Marchandaise'. We had furries†served out here, were bundled into wagons, 26 in each, and after emergency rations and rations for the journey were served out we started off.

We came across in a cattle boat, were fed on cattle biscuits, wore cattle coats and now we're driven in a cattle wagon. Some 25 hours of this, crushed and cramped, dozing on straw for a few minutes, coming back to consciousness frozen. We had a vile, undrinkable mixture when we halted in a siding for a few minutes, made of rum and coffee, unsweetened and cold. Still we recovered our spirits and landed in Cassel about 9 o'clock in the morning. We passed Rouen and Calais en route. The country as a whole, flat. The farmhouses surrounded by a grassy rampart surmounted by tall trees pruned to the trunk. A plan learned, I think, in warfare as every farm or hamlet is thus defensible. The roads are lined with the same tall trees filing along two deep. The

---

* Reference to the work of the French satirical poet Nicholas Boileau.
† Overcoat made from goat or sheepskin.

orchards are plentiful, trees dressed by the left. A very pretty countryside to spend a holiday in, on a bicycle.

We had a hurried meal at Cassel. Bob G, Dan McK and I had a glass of coffee and bread with butter in a café, very good, all at 2d a time, daintily served in a pretty room heated by a huge stove. There we fell in, coats on, on our back our pack, blanket, furry and mess tin. You'd think they collected all the hills in France and planted them round Cassel. We trudged along, Colonel and an interpreter at the head on horses. We had a rest every three or four miles for a minute or two, then over the rough causeway and mud through Steenvorde, L'Abeele and Boeschepe to Poperinghe.

We were quartered in farm buildings round about as dusk was falling. It was dark when we got a share of hot water to make oxo. The star shells could be seen dropping over the trenches about four miles off, then to a blessed sleep in the straw till next morning. Only wakened once with cold which was soon remedied. We – Bill and I – had most of our clothes off. What ho.

## ~ *Shrines and Wreaths* ~

L'Abeele
Tuesday, 2nd March

Brilliant morning after a sound rest. Settling down to write after a refreshing wash up.

While I remember, the roads are causewayed only in the centre, about a cart's breadth, the margins being knee deep in mud in soft weather. Every half mile or so a shrine is met, sometimes only a thing like a dovecot hung in a tree, usually a wood hut with an altar inside on which stands a crucifix, a favourite saint or two, the Madonna and Child and the candles. Occasionally a wooden crucifix about life-size is met, carved very expertly.

Almost all the women when dressed on Sunday were draped in

black; a little cemetery at Boeschepe, crowded with wreaths, tells why. We are allowed into the village in parties for a short time but all must carry a rifle and five rounds in case a sniper is met.

## ~ *A Café* ~

L'Abeele
Wednesday, 3rd March

Rising after a light sleep.

Jiny, Bill S., Bill J. and I had an hour or so in the village yesterday afternoon. We sat in a café, drank coffee and beer, parlez-voused with the women who were serving and became interested in the host's little girl, a sober, sweet-faced maid of fourteen. I carried on a conversation partly in French aided with the little English she understood. She said Carrie was 'jolie' but didn't think the photograph like me at all.

The Germans came to this village one night; two men were shot, provisions were demanded in the café at the point of the revolver. The little girl fled with the others, returning when the Huns had fled before the Allied soldiers.

## ~ *Rehearsals and Rum* ~

L'Abeele
Friday, 5th March

Wednesday and Thursday evenings from 6.30 onwards for a few hours were spent rehearsing the relieving of trenches, flopping down flat in the gluey mud every time a signal went signifying the bursting of a star shell. The real thing was seen on the horizon, the shells lighting up the night to a white glow and the guns booming dully.

Bryce and I were detailed to act as guides last night.[42] It was a godsend to have a temporary elevation from being a human machine and use a little initiative. The notorious tot of rum is served each night but I used it only on Wednesday and then only watered down.

## ~ *Under Fire* ~

Dickebusch
Monday, 15th March

Left our billets near Poperinghe last Friday and marched through Boeschepe and Reninghelst to a little clump of trees near Dickebusch. Among the trees are set some 60 little tents like Indian wigwams. In these we've since been settled with additional companies coming at intervals.

Every night since we came till last night we've been under fire while digging reserve trenches and only had two wounded. Last night B and D companies were booked for the fire trenches but the German artillery was playing hell, making it impossible to relieve C Company who were in along with the 1st Royal Scots.

Stood by for a while and, after more rations were sent to C Company, we lay down, ready at a moment's notice to take the road. Our artillery belched replies all night and musketry barking. We, the British, lost four trenches and recaptured three. This is the net result meantime of Hindenburg's effort to reach Calais by the 15th March.

Their artillery was like themselves, any amount of bark but no great bite. They ripped an observation mound to bits and tore up some reserve trenches, but their infantry attack petered out. Our lads didn't worry at the prospect of bloody butchery last night. We can rough it hard when it's needed, but in the present circumstances a little more grub would leave us less hungry and these damned Belgians fleece us at every opportunity. I'm certain that Dickebusch is full of pro-Germans and that they give away information as the price of their safety. The friction would be eased if the authorities had the horse-sense to open a regimental canteen. A temporary affair on wheels run by an honest contractor would pay both him and us.

Had a pleasant debate last night starting with Germany and ending with Trades Unionism versus Socialism. The debate ended with the candle.

## ~ *Canadian Light Infantry* ~

Dickebusch
Monday evening, 15th March

Getting ready to go into the trenches; the 'Princess Pats' are a game lot. Went into battle last night with cigs between their teeth. It's at a time like this that a little bucks you up though.

## ~ *Running the Gauntlet* ~

Dickebusch
Monday, 22nd March

Events follow each other so quickly, and each wild experience is swallowed up by a later one still more exciting, that what happened only last week is as distant as last year.

Well, last Monday, so far as I can remember, all B Company paraded with water bottles filled and twenty-four hours' haversack rations, with waterproof sheets and teddy bear coats tied on our backs and marched off. On the road a couple of shells burst about 50 yards away with a white flash and a deafening report. Then after being detailed off in squads we started to creep to the trenches through hedges, floundering through ditches and shell holes, flares lighting up the dark and showing us up to a hellish hail of bullets but, by the mercy of God, although the lead rang on the rifles and kicked the earth at our head, we ran the gauntlet to trench No. 8, 130 yards or so from the German lines held, I believe, by Bavarians.

When under direct fire all your control is needed to lie dead quiet. For myself, I confess, I breathed a verse about 'Stammering Sam'.* I felt an impulse to rise from the mud and run for a deep, deep hole.

## ~ *First Casualties* ~

Dickebusch
Tuesday, 23rd March

To continue. During the night one of every three men takes a turn for an hour peeping over the sandbag breastwork, shooting and ducking when a flare looks like silhouetting him as a target. Owing to ours being an advanced trench, there was a danger of enfilade fire, so smoking and noise were forbidden.

The position roughly was this. Night quickly gave place to dawn and the scene was dismal. A few dead cows or horses lying about, the cunning trenches opposite a silent menace, separated only by a rickle of barbed wire and a sprint. Behind our trench were a few graves and crosses. Among them, to my surprise and pain, was Sergeant Chrichton, the first to go west of our battalion.

Though small, the 'traversed' breastwork was very comfortable and the day would have been monotonous but for the Germans shelling our reserve trenches, our guns ploughing up the mound at St Eloi away to our left and a sniper rasping away the top of the parapet and throwing the dirt over my book and down my neck.

---

* From a popular song of the same name composed by Abbie Senter. Beatson is referring to the second verse:

> I s-s-s-slither and s-s-s-slide
> Whenever I move awound
> I'm s-s-s-sneaky and s-s-s-sly
> 'Cause I always lie flat on the gwound
> I'm s-s-s-slender and s-s-s-slim
> Enormously gifted with gwace
> I'm s-s-s-sleek and I'm s-s-s-swift
> I can vanish without any twace.

Night fell and we were relieved and returned to the wood and slept. Since then I, along with varying numbers, have been either digging trenches, building sandbag parapets or putting up barbed wire entanglements. Bryce and I have acted as guides. Sergeant Thompson was good enough to compliment me on my work on Friday last. We have been having it pretty hot at times; Jameson hit on the hip and Dryburgh on the forehead in our little party. When we get to point blank range, 400 yards or under, it is best to keep crouching though not seen as the bullet fired from the shoulder, if it finds its billet, finds it in the head or breast. Last night, while a few of us were carrying rations to D Company in the reserve trenches, young Bennett fell hit in the forehead two paces in front of me. Just a flutter and another lad gone west.

On getting back to billets I heard that Macdonald was hit in the breast today. His sergeant tells me he died soon after. I'm on easy terms with death but it's damnable to be hit in the dark by a sniping cur. My heart is sore for the lads and their folks. God pity us.

Today we're moving somewhere else. In the lull of preparations I've at last got my narrative up to date.

### ~ *The Belgian Countryside* ~

Mt Kokereel
Wednesday, 24th March

Next scene, a hayloft standing back from a very second class road. Time: after breakfast, weather bright with light showers. Marched here from the wood where it's 'Verboten ingang', back the roads we travelled on Friday the 12th, through Reninghelst and skirting Westoutre some ten miles or so.

It would have been delightful to sit at the foot of one of the tall straight trees that line the avenue, the white crescent of the moon shining through light clouds, the flat country melting in the haze and shadows of trees dimly seen, sit and dream of an island washed by the

Southern Pacific, the haze of its waters surrounding all and 'Uma' coming gliding down the avenue or the sailor reeling along with the 'Bottle Imp'* in one hand and the brandy in the other. The scene would have pleased Stevenson and thousands more, a poem by nature. It made one forget the gnawing of my shoulder straps.

Should God spare me, this country will see me again. I want to hear wooden sabots clattering over its cobbles and see the avenues with the homeward bound workers in the evening and its 'estaminets' brilliantly lit and peopled with a noisy debating group such as only villages produce. Children and mothers at the doors or in the gardens. See it at daybreak, noon, evening and moonlight and you'll feel the peace of the country. May the day soon come when its ruins will be restored and its peoples return to it.

## ~ The War May Soon Be Over ~

Ypres
Monday, 29th March

My tongue isn't the pen of a ready writer so justice will not be done to the record of impressions received in this little room of the 'Abbaye Royale des Benedictine Irlandaises, Ypres'.[43]

Since arriving here last Friday there has been a hot hunt for souvenirs.[44] The place was littered with rubbish, old letters, accounts dated 1790, religious tracts and endless variety of odds and ends. Occupied by Germans for a few days, then by French troops, then British cavalry and now by us. After, we made it habitable with water and disinfectant following the traditional habits of British soldiers. Pictures on all sides show ghastly hearts dripping with blood and flaming, encircled with a wreath of roses. The endless variation on that theme is depressing and the thought of girls spending the bloom

---

* 'Uma' and 'The Bottle Imp' are references to two short stories, 'The Beach of Falasa' and 'The Bottle Imp', by Robert Louis Stevenson, first published in 1893 in the collection *Island Nights' Entertainment* (also known as *South Sea Tales*).

of youth contemplating such is repulsive to my mind. But I found here a letter written by a girl in Coventry to the Right Hon. Lady Abbess which breathed with religion, the sincerity of which was touching and would have been a masterpiece for a Hall Caine novel, but with those perpetual reminders of death and the cry of Pax on the walls (when there is no peace) a laugh must seem criminal. Many a time the floor I stand on must have been wet with tears of remorse and sorrow and the heartbrokenness of girls who should be laughing and brightening this too gray world.

The town itself has suffered terribly from shellfire especially but cafés still trade and stalls line the pavements. French soldiers are resting and very interesting to talk to although laborious. Good-hearted fellows. One's an advocate in the 68th Regiment and gave an interesting half-hour in a café today. Speaking pretty good English, he said, 'You English at St Eloi lose seven trenches. Joffre say to your General French "I give you a new division". French says "No, we lose trenches we take them again", so English take seven trenches and once more we say English good', quite alright. In his opinion the war may finish any day now as the Germans are greatly outnumbered and their great power lies in their machine-guns now. He gave the news that Holland had declared war. I've got an enhanced opinion of the French after what he told me.

Since arriving here we've only been up to the reserve trenches once, on Saturday night, quite safe too, no bullets flying around, about 2,000 yards behind the fire trenches.

Very cold at nights sleeping on wooden floors.

~ *'La Belle Alliance'* ~

Ypres
Tuesday, 30th March

I ought to have mentioned the good time spent with the French soldiers in the café on Sunday night. A sergeant, Allouis Julien of the

1$^{ier}$ Cie [*First Company*] 68th Regiment d'Infantrie, Section Postal 66, gave me his rosary as a keepsake. Jolly fine company, ten in all, treated Watson and I to white wine galore. I met a few of the same lot last night and only lack of time made us part. We always tinkle our glasses to 'La Belle Alliance' and leave each other with a handshake and a salaam. Only one drawback to their character is their inbred viciousness.

Disease is rampant in Ypres; some half dozen cafés have been put out of bounds for us. I suppose lack of doctors prevents proper supervision.

Last night we marched to the same line of trenches we worked on Saturday night; their formation is novel like this.* The advantages are protection from the backward effect of shrapnel fire with easy evacuation and re-entrance into the fire trench should the shells be landed accurately. The excavation behind breastwork A being about 3ft deep also enables relieving to be done safer.

### ~ *Windmills* ~

Ypres
Wednesday, 31st March

Just came off guard at 3 p.m. today. A good feed and a wash set me on my legs again. The feed nothing very elaborate, in a house–café, cost for two: 3fr 20c.† Looks as if the close approaching new generation were being prepared for. The vendors, one bright specimen sporting a souvenir in hiding, are at the same game, everything double its value; still, it's excusable all things considered.

One feature of the place I've neglected to mention are the windmills set on every hill. Picturesque, one outside the town has been demolished by shell fire. Verb. sap.‡

---

* As referred to in the Editors' Note, Beatson apparently intended to add a diagram at a later date; see also the entry for 30 April.

† 3 francs 20 centimes, at the time equivalent to a little less than 3 shillings.

‡ *Verbum sapienti*: a word to the wise is enough.

April 1915

*The 9th Royal Scots were stationed at Vlamertinghe, one mile west of Ypres, when the Second Battle of Ypres commenced with heavy German shelling. '[They] watched the pall of smoke that lay over the town, and presently the eastern sky was bright with the flames of burning buildings.'⁴⁵ C and D Companies supported the Duke of Cornwall's Light Infantry while Beatson's B Company, along with A Company, supported the Canadians' heroic defence of the front line near St Julien, a feat that was widely credited with preventing a German victory. The Regimental War Diary records 25 killed, 177 wounded and 10 missing or taken prisoner during April. At the start of the battle, on 22 April, the Royal Scots witnessed the infamous first use of poison gas by the Germans.*

~ *Correspondence* ~

Ypres
Thursday, 1st April

A brilliant day, spending it lying on the grassy slopes of the ramparts and mustering energy and words to answer Carrie's letter. I am in clover today, have received three letters and one P.P.C. [*picture postcard*], and parcels aren't in yet. Internal mechanism doctored up with castor oil and laudanum, a fiendish mixture. Popping away as usual at aeros, one passing overhead is pure white and almost invisible against the blue sky.

Later same day

We've had a rest from digging tonight which has given me the opportunity of writing Carrie and her father, my father and Bella. A parcel from Bella arrived about 6.30, so Watson and I had oxo for supper. Trés bon!

'**Our dug-out, that is Watson and I, was only about 3ft high.**' 'Casino', a support line dug-out in the Bois Grenier sector.

'**Shifted again last night back to our old dug-outs in the Sanctuary Wood.**' A communication trench linking the front line ('fire trench') and reserve trenches, Sanctuary Wood, June 1915.

**'French soldiers are resting and very interesting to talk to although laborious.'** Soldiers from the French 7th Infantry.

**'She is an exceptional specimen of the refugee species in this village.'** A Belgian soldier looking after refugees.

'Today I've spent cleaning myself; just had a shave and a wash-up, cleaned my rifle and bayonet.' Men of the 9th Royal Scots shaving, or at least pretending to shave, with bayonets.

'The fumes are horrible and hang in the air for a long time.' The primitive but quite effective form of protection against gas worn by Argyll and Sutherland Highlanders in this May 1916 photograph was soon replaced by a more sophisticated gas mask with a variety of filters.

**'I was called out again last night to guide a stretcher party to the dressing station.'** The 18th Field Ambulance dressing station at Vlamertinghe, June 1915.

**'Things have been quiet as far as big fighting goes but there is a steady dribble of casualties.'** No. 10 casualty clearing station at L'Abeele.

'I saw the wounded on all sides.  I did what little I could but it is heart-rending to hear the fellows asking for help and see the dead lying so very still.' British doctor and padre attending to wounded British and German soldiers.

'We waited till dusk and guided stretcher parties.' Walking wounded wheeling back a stretcher case on a child's perambulator.

'The roads are causewayed in the centre, about a cart's breadth, the margins being knee deep in mud in soft weather.' A water-cart stuck in mud to the axle, one wheel and one horse having gone over the edge of the brushwood track, 1917.

'Horses were lying at the roadside dead and dying.' Half of the one million horses used by the British Army were killed by gun and shellfire; most of those that survived the war were sold to the French as food to avoid the expense of transporting them back to Britain.

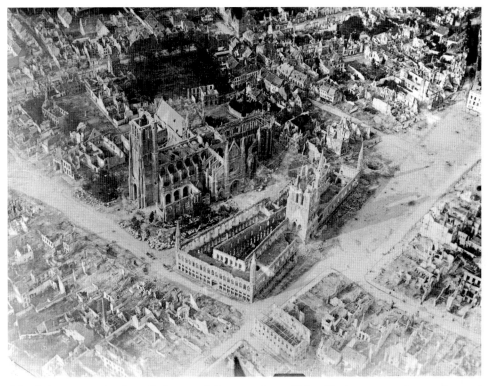

'The brimstone rained on Sodom and Gomorrah could hardly have caused more havoc.' Aerial view of Ypres, 1915.

'What a paradise lost . . . the shattered walls of a once splendid chateau, the tumbledown statuary and fountains.' The ruins of Hooge Chateau in early 1915; it would later be completely destroyed during the Second Battle of Ypres.

**'The camp was in a grass field between Reninghelst and Poperinghe, a bivouac being made with "cabers" and blankets.'** Tents and bivouacs in a rest field near Poperinghe, June 1915.

**'A column of buses drew up and we had a welcome drive back.'** London double-decker buses being used to transport troops.

## ~ *God's Will* ~

Good Friday! Has mankind any heart or brain? Are we too utterly dense and blind to the greatest good? Then well may God give us up to a brutish death at our brother's hands. But no! As we are made in the image of God I believe we're doing His will in crushing this big bellied military force. But again, the Kaiser claims the alliance of God sincerely or insincerely. Or is this God dispassionately feeding His earth with men?

## ~ *Easter Egg* ~

Ypres
Saturday, 3rd April

Received another letter from Bella with the tidings that an Easter egg will be mine on Sunday. Received it yesterday alone in its splendid isolation.[46] Went out digging at 8 o'clock last night, black as pitch, returned shortly after 12 o'clock this morning.

## ~ *Wet, Muddy and Cold* ~

Hooge
Tuesday, 6th April

Eleven o'clock at night sitting in a dug-out, my back to a fire and a candle, with rapid fire rattling about 500 yards away and shots whining anxiously past overhead; with shells occasionally soaring over the treetops and bursting a little away, here sit I – but I'll start my tale of woe from the beginning.

On Saturday night I was detailed by Caldwell (CURSE HIM) to

form one of the carrying party going some six miles out to a dumping station with barbed wire, fascines\*, etc., etc. We paraded at 4.20 p.m., landing back about 2 a.m. next morning – drenched to the skin and plastered with mud. In the interval the damned inevitable muddle kept us waiting at a roadside, in a trench, moving six yards in as many minutes, without guides. Left us five hours to get giddy with cold, cower for shelter and try to draw heat from each other. All we could do we did, curse the incompetency of pothouse lawyers. In revenge praised the French method of drawing their officers from the ranks. We regained our spirits a little going home and managed to raise a song. As I tumbled into bed I promised myself a long sleep into the afternoon.

Lord pity me? That morning after breakfast Captain Bell popped his head round the door and with a consoling grin said that guides were to parade at 11 o'clock for A & B Companies under Captains Ferguson and Blair. Full marching order, so it was Au Revoir to the convent.

## ~ Description of Dug-outs ~

Hooge
Wednesday, 7th April

To continue. We set out with seven guides, three N.C.O.s, two Captains and a mounted interpreter. Steady slogging to a dumping station at the end of a road at Dead Man's Bottom Wood, then taking notes for guiding. We passed through what had once been a beautiful estate with a large pond, wooded and shrubbery round a ruined chateau close to Hooge. Then a little further to the Sanctuary Wood where our dug-outs were located.

From the dumping station to our dug-outs was honeycombed with

---

\* Pipes or bundles of sticks used to lay over barbed wire or ditches to enable a crossing to be made.

dug-outs occupied by Frenchmen. Their huts are comfortable or cramped for height according to the inmate, some are only 3ft high, others 6ft with fireplaces, ledges cut out and ornamented. All are concealed in the wood with brushwood on the roofs. We spent the day gassing and gourmandering with the Frenchies and at night we went to the dumping station for the companies, brought them here and just as we were entering the wood, a shell tore towards but burst high about 100 yards away. Our dug-out, that is Watson and I, was only about 3ft high with a fireplace but we deepened it yesterday to 5ft and improved the drainage etc, etc. The place was filthy with refuse left by the Froggies. The dug-outs vary in size, some hold 17 down to two, the general is about five.

On Monday night again guides were called out to go to the dumping station just as I was settling down to sleep. The usual party got lost, we wandered about in the dark till we got them, or rather they wandered to us. Returned about three hours later after hiding the cargo which couldn't be carried.

On Friday I was informed that guides were declared off all duties and fatigues, which sort of balances matters as I was called out again last night to guide a stretcher party to the dressing station. Bryce shot in the foot with his own rifle,[47] Lance Corporal Chisholm shot in the left hand. Three others were shot in the camping party last night, I hear, and a working party were up at the fire trenches, but I know not how they fared. This part of the line is a devil for sapping and mining from what I hear from the R.I.F. [*Royal Inniskilling Fusiliers*] who are holding it; will find out for ourselves shortly.

Today I've spent cleaning myself; just had a shave and a wash-up, cleaned my rifle and bayonet and now Watson is trying to improve the fireplace and dry the floor with ashes and sand. We dug rather deeply yesterday and the water was squelching on the floor under the sheets this morning. It's a nuisance always lifting the tail of your kilt when you go in. The guns are going ahead all round this quarter and Hooge shows the effect of the German replies. Houses wrecked to a brick.

I forgot to mention I had a letter and two papers from Bella and a letter from Carrie yesterday morning. Oh that they were longer but they were welcome all right.

## ~ *All The Kaiser's Fault* ~

Hooge
Thursday, 8th April

Out with a carrying party last night, ankle deep in mud to dug-outs occupied by the 9th A.&S.H. [*Argyll & Sutherland Highlanders*] lying in support of two of their own companies in the firing line. Dug-outs in a wood swept by bullets and shells.

Came back to a miserable night's rest, floor flooded, wakened every little while frozen to the heart and cramp in both legs. Crawled out and had a heat at the Sergeant Major's fire while sorting letters for him.

This morning the weather is unsettled, fair and hail time about and chilly especially when there's no dry wood to raise a flame in our mud hut. Oh for ten minutes in front of the fire at home with a wash up in warm water and able to stand up without bringing down an avalanche of dirt all over you and your kit. Tea and dirt tastes rotten. I've never felt in so rotten a humour since we reached France as this morning. Damn the Kaiser and curse his breed forever. Amen.

Later same day

I should note the burst of rapid fire on our front yesterday. It was prolonged and brought the order to 'Stand To' Full Marching Order; still to learn the result.

Our dug-outs being so verminous, the blankets haven't been given us, so we retire thusly – socks on, kilt loosened, jacket buttoned only at the waist, greatcoat turned upside down and legs slid into the sleeves. This leaves you to curl up and chew the mud off the foot of the coat.

## ~ *More Correspondence* ~

Glencorse Wood
Friday, 9th April

Yesterday afternoon we had a cosy fire in our dug-out. Envelopes for private correspondence had been served out, four per man per month, so I settled down and broke records in writing. A letter to Carrie and a note to her Dad ran me into nine pages, which relieved my mind a great deal.

About 8 o'clock we paraded Full Marching Order, guides in front, and travelled to the dug-outs in a wood which lies in support to trenches Nos 67 to 73, No. 73 being the trench allotted to No. 8 platoon. The Company Guides for A & B Companies met the guides for the 1st A.&S.H. and when C & D Companies arrived from Ypres about 10 p.m. we led them to their respective trenches.

The line we occupy is easy for entrance and exit and strongly supported by machine-guns, but more of that when our turn comes. We got back in the morning and lay down through force of habit and because it's customary to do it at night-time, but we wakened frozen meat when the effect of the rum faded away; it's always the feet that trouble you. Anyhow, it made up for the lot when I got a letter from Carrie, one from Nan, a P.C. [*postcard*] from Jessie and papers from Bella – all this morning.

## ~ *A Close Shave* ~

Glencorse Wood
Saturday, 10th April

Spent yesterday wandering about the wood here, looking for curios. In this wood called Glencorse Wood was fought the famous battle of Ypres.[48] Our progress can be traced by the dug-outs and shallow trenches every five yards or so, every foot has been contested. The equipments, caps, jackets and ammunition lying about among the brushwood tell of lives lost. Lieutenant Stewart took Watson and I up to Fitzclarence Farm near our artillery observation post from where we could see our trenches but no Huns. It appears that we are holding part of the Territorial sector and that at present the Germans are not in great force on our front.[49]

Yesterday a Lieutenant, a Corporal and eight men of C Company were wounded by shrapnel in their trenches and a Private of A Company killed while working behind the trenches last night. Watson and I led Lieutenant Smith-Grant up to Trench 73 last night and back again while the rest of the section replaced the casualties in C Company. While 'running' for water this forenoon, McKay, Hepburn and I were sniped at, close shaves but 'a miss is as good as a mile'.

The weather today is promising well for our spell of the trenches; we go in tonight.

## ~ *A French Soldier's Skeleton* ~

Vlamertinghe
Tuesday, 13th April

While waiting for tea I'll finish my story. We went to Trench 72 at dusk on Saturday night heavily loaded. Night very chilly. Sunday: warm night as usual, prolonged bursts of rapid fire on our left kept us on the 'qui vive'.* Monday morning while having breakfast about 6 o'clock Scott and Lyon were hit in the head by a sniper. Jock [*Scott*] was also hit in the hand, both pretty bad. Watson and I crawled to camp to try and get relief for them, but that not being procurable, we waited till dusk and guided stretcher parties.

We guides were kept busy at times and we have to be slick to slip the Huns; rather go up to my knees in water than show my headpiece.

In a communication trench I crept through the skeleton of a

---

\* 'Who goes there?'; to be 'on the qui vive' means constantly on the alert for enemy attack.

Frenchman that was lying beneath the water, the white bones sticking out of his tunic, poor chap. 'Our Father which art in Heaven.' Scots, French, Germans, Austrians, Russians and the rest, return to 'our' Mother Earth, groaning and cursing.

We were relieved last night, dragged ourselves for eight miles to the little wooden hut at Vlamertinghe. Slept from about 5 this morning until 2 in the afternoon, the first for three days or more, and we had our clothes off and a blanket each so our sleep was sound. Wakened to receive a parcel from Carrie, her mother has blessings showered on her.

## ~ *Superior German Trenches* ~

Vlamertinghe
Wednesday, 14th April

The narrative stopped short last night as tea arrived and lights were ordered out before we had finished. In future all lights have to be out at 9 p.m. This is in consequence of an airship dropping bombs on Monday night about 100 yards from the huts. Six in all were dropped, but only two were anything near. They made the huts sway, I hear. Everybody was scared at the terrific report and the holes they dug show they ain't just crackers.

Last night I went for a chat into the village, had coffee and wine and jawed with the fellows. One of 'Princess Pats' got my shoulder till a 'Cheshire' spoke well for the 'French Foreign Legion', 75% of which are wanted by police, all nations under the sun are in it. Came back to tea, had biscuits and cake to it. 'Trés bon mes beaux enfants.'

A word or two about the Germans who oppose us. Their fire trenches are believed to be on our half right and half left with a communication trench between. They held a wood on our half right and ruins in front. Between us they had dummy trenches, a hedge at an angle and their proper trench was decorated with dummy loopholes*. They weren't in great force but they were 'Bisleys'† and our procedure and trenches were childish in comparison. We had a wood at our back, a few ruins, we had marksmen and though we outnumbered them, they easily had the superiority of fire because we hadn't the horse-sense to use our advantages. We were so silly as to have all our loopholes stuffed and in a trench with breastwork about 6ft high we had no head cover but had to fire over the parapet. We British are game to the last, but damned stupid at times, and this was one such time last weekend.

### ~ *Parcels, Pluck and Patience* ~

Vlamertinghe
Thursday, 15th April

What a time we had yesterday with our long looked for parcels, two from Bella and a letter from Carrie. Everybody was pressing cake on each other but I bet none was like the one Carrie's Ma made. It gives me 'that tired feeling'‡ to think of trenches and bully beef and biscuits, but I'm carrying some of the treasure trove back although I've to crawl with it. Met a Portobello chum last night in an éstaminet.

Today is a glorious example of what a summer day should be. Aeros are flitting about like butterflies. It was against the grain to do 2¼ hours drill but our 'al fresco' dinner made up for it. Melton Mowbray pie, pineapple, cake, dates and chocolate sitting on a blanket in the sun.

Had word this morning of desperate attacks by the Schwein-Huns at St Eloi repulsed heavily. Our artillery went ding-dong from midnight. Heard from a Lance Corporal in D Company who got

---

* Holes made through the parapet through which to fire without having to raise one's head above the parapet.
† Slang for 'the real thing' from a contemporary advertisement.
‡A line from a popular tune.

through the shelling at Ypres that the three shells landed from different directions. A fellow in French officer's uniform was taking note of the damage shortly after and on being accosted by a French officer merely nodded. Investigation succeeded suspicion and he proved to be a German in disguise; another seven were rooted out in the same fashion.

It's only too true that we're fighting at present with kid gloves on, while the Huns are going at it tooth and nail. We need pluck, patience and a pair of glasses for the snipers and the cunning of the Devil himself for them all, all the time.

## ~ Anticipating a Big Attack ~

Ypres
Friday, 16th April

As I was writing Bella last night the word flew round to pack up immediately. Underclothing, etc., had to go to make room for the parcels and even then some were left. As we lay on the parade ground Lieutenant Stewart called for Watson and I and the three of us went ahead to Ypres to look for billets for the battalion which followed 15 minutes later. It seemed we were to follow up in 'close support' as a big attack by us was anticipated, so all night we lay with everything ready. The billets we got were quite close to the Benedictine Convent and had just been vacated by the 18th Royal Irish.

We rose this morning about 8 o'clock after a comfortable night on the straw and Watson and I went out to a café and had a tuck in to coffee and buttered rolls. On coming out I stood at a stall to buy a few P.P.C.s when again the word was passed that we were shifting. Luckily only a short distance this time to other billets where we are staying for the day.

The sun is bright and warm so I'm doing the daily diary on the grassy green.

## ~ *Stood To Arms* ~

Glencorse Wood
Sunday, 18th April

On Friday night we trekked along the railway back to the dug-outs arriving early on Saturday morning; Sellars being detailed as the new guide along with myself. Watson being an N.C.O. returns to his section. C & D Companies with a few of our company continued to the trenches.

On Saturday there was some liveliness in our artillery on our right. We 'Stood to Arms' but no movement was made in our sector. On Saturday night at 9 p.m. I reported myself to the 'Orderly Room' but not until 11 o'clock was I needed to guide a party of the Adjutant, Brigade Major, Engineer Captain and Sergeant on a tour of inspection round trenches 69 to 73. The Major's criticism was sharp and unsparing, gave as much information in five minutes as would take five months and your life to find out. The adjutant and your humble returned to the dug-outs at 3.15 this morning in time for the 'Stand To' at dawn.

I mustn't omit the fact that I've sent away 13 postcards in two days, three yesterday, ten today and received word from Bella, Mr Sponder and Jim Sanderson.

# Part II:

# The Second Battle of Ypres and its Aftermath

*~ Heavy Shelling of Ypres ~*

Vlamertinghe
Wednesday, 21st April

Back in Vlamertinghe, bright day with a sharp wind blowing. We landed about 4 o'clock this morning and since then I've been sleeping and eating. It's best to do both when one has the chance, whether you're sleepy or hungry or whether you're not, for one never knows when you're getting the next sleep or meal.

We went into the trenches last Sunday night and were relieved last night, Tuesday, having a quiet time in the interval; no casualties in our Company. These last two days Ypres has been heavily shelled and it continues; batteries are shelling all five entrances and indiscriminately in the town itself. Last night we got through quite safely but saw the ghastly evidences on the streets. The motive for shelling at this particular time may be the knowledge that only British troops are now occupying the town, their partiality for us over our allies is well known, or else the setback they received last Saturday and Sunday when we took Hill 60 from them.[50] This hill lies to the right of our sector, north-east of Ypres.

Various little incidents have been occurring which would have been worth mentioning one time but familiarity has bred contempt. What is more important is an engine puffing on the railway nearby, four beautiful, if dirty, calves grazing beside me; it's a real mental tonic to see them.

## ~ *The Western Front* ~

Vlamertinghe
Thursday, 22nd April

Received parcels from Bella and Miss Alston[51] yesterday. Bella's of café au lait and Miss Alston's half dozen hankies being especially welcome.

This morning is much warmer and brighter than yesterday and am setting to write after the rifle inspection, lying in a hamlet in a blanket on the grass. I read an illuminating article by one who knows in this week's 'Weekly Dispatch'. He dealt with 2½ millions of Germans holding our front in the west. The length of the front, about 600 miles, allows a thin firing line of 1,000,000, the same number in reserve and about 500,000 details which augurs well for a successful offensive shortly.

Later same day

O you who sit secure in England complacent in your armchairs and jar at Germany, would lose some of your gawky cockiness if you saw the wringing of hands and the terror-stricken looks of the Belgians here when the alarm came an hour ago of a French retiral beyond Ypres. The hubbub started as I sat writing in a café. A crowd were outside watching our artillery making excellent practice on a German aeroplane, it was making along our left when I got out, dropping fuses as it went. Then French artillery from the firing line, weary and battered, hurried through the village.

## ~ *The Battle* ~

Sanctuary Wood
Thursday, 29th April

As I was saying last week – if some of the men in the homeland could see and feel, their heads would come off their chests and their hands off their bellies. The French, black and white,[52] both alike grimy, the mules straining as the guns clattered back, we stood to and moved off at night. That night we spent in a field but we were early on the move again, as ignorant of why and wherefore as the 'men' in a game of draughts.

We spent part of the forenoon squatting in Pottige [*Potijze*] Wood with Canadian batteries barking all about us and the German shells wrecking the farmhouses and laying out the gunners. The whole air was electrified with the expectation of blood flowing.

Again on the move along the road parallel to the German line. The shrapnel started coming over, 20 of our men were hit at Whichy [*Wieltje*]. Houses and cafés deserted all along the road, bottles and glasses, wine and beer, left in the flight. We rushed up in small parties along the road, across fields under shellfire all the way to St Julien. Closer than we then knew to the Germans but being unsupported we, only two platoons of us at one point, gathered and went back safely this time to Whichy. There the two companies, after getting bandoliers standing in the lee of the end house, rushed across a field by sections.

The succeeding events were alternating rushes and rests, shrapnel and stink bombs, bursting and sickening us with poisonous fumes and inflaming our eyes. Our artillery seemed miserably inadequate. I only wish the fellows who grumble at home over a few coppers or hours overtime were sent out here; they would understand things a bit better from our point of view.

These stink bombs have only a local explosive effect, our Lieutenant Stewart being only bowled over by one bursting six feet away, but the fumes are horrible and hang in the air for a long time. The last part of the journey up we came under hot fire, the ground spurting up all round but C & D Companies on our left were harder hit than we were. When at last we stopped behind a hedge we hurriedly dug ourselves in to get head cover at least. That night when on a manage back* to the Colonel, I saw the wounded on all sides. I did what little I could but it is heart-rending to hear the fellows asking for help and see the dead lying so very still.

The following day we had no rations sent us, our 'emergencies' were done. Sellars and I got water at Pottige Chateau for the platoon. On the road, the German shells were making brick-dust of the houses. I found some sugar and cold chocolate in a café which had just been deserted; that disappeared. One pathetic incident was a goat that saw Lieutenant Sellars and I as we made our way through the ruins of a farm. It came running towards us like a frightened child and followed us till dusk when we got rid of it at the farm on our road back. Cows wandered about our trenches heavy with milk and bewildered. I managed to creep out and get a pint or so of milk but, being spotted, put an end to the game.

Digging and trekking from dawn to dusk, with little to eat or drink till we were withdrawn to the dug-outs we made in Pottige Wood where we spent a night and a day. We left on the second night in the wood, the Lieutenant, myself and three others in advance, leaving behind us freshly made and cooked stew that had been dispatched by us from our own woks. You have to feel hungry for a few days to appreciate this disaster.

Our Lieutenant Stewart made us sweat till we got to the 81st Brigade Headquarters where we received directions from General Croker for the distribution of the battalion. One company was sent to the 'Tank' [*drinks canteen*], one to Polygon Wood and A & B companies to Sanctuary Wood here, a little to the north-west of our previous dug-outs. After arriving yesterday morning we slept long

---

* Slang term for 'acting as guide'.

and deeply till afternoon, rose, got a cat's wash and basked in the sun.

Today is splendid and so hot that a few of us went to a shallow and muddy brook and bathed. Butterflies are flitting about, an aeroplane dropping sinister fuses only suggests to our drowsy minds a droning bee. The cuckoo is calling and altogether the wood is delightful, so much so that Bill Swan, Percy Telford and I lay under a pine tree and recalled bygone days of happiness spent in the country. It strikes a sweet note to recall the heather hills and good times at 'Achae [*Scotland*].

The sun is now sinking slowly and a cool breeze is stirring the trees. What horrible mockery that the peace of nature should be broken by the blast of cannon and whizzing of stray bullets and the thought of men having to die for the liberty to govern themselves. Never mind, God's in His Heaven,* keep looking up.


## ~ *Hooge Chateau* ~

Sanctuary Wood
Friday, 30th April

Shifted again last night back to our old dug-outs in the Sanctuary Wood. A party of us went digging trenches today in the grounds of the Hooge Chateau. What a paradise lost – the apple- and pear-blossomed trees, the delicate pink and white Japanese maple. The fresh greenery and cool shade and long avenue contrast with the shattered walls of a once splendid chateau, the tumbledown statuary and fountains. Sun was blazing warm, ideal for a summer picnic. I could almost imagine I was digging in the garden on my summer holidays.

The line of the trenches, if occupied, would blunt the too acute angle of our firing line at this point. Although it would mean the yielding of ground, it would make the position safer to my mind. The position is roughly this. The dotted portion is the line under

---

* Quote from Robert Browning's *Pippa Passes*.

construction at this point.[53] From all accounts our work last Friday had a greater moral effect on the situation than we imagined; our appearance as reinforcements stayed the attacks of the Germans though we didn't have a shot at them.[54]

It is almost 8 o'clock and getting too dark to write. It is a beautifully calm evening and I intend spending the night under this tree.

May 1915

*The Second Battle of Ypres continued until 25 May. For most of the month the battalion manned front-line trenches near Hooge, suffering further casualties: 17 killed and 83 wounded.*

## ~ *Sulphurous Fumes* ~

Sanctuary Wood
Sunday, 2nd May

Yesterday was May Day. I woke wet with May dew. It was a glorious day. Road in front was shelled in the evening and we were almost suffocated with sulphurous fumes. Wrote Carrie, Jim Sanderson, John Alston and another.

Today is duller with a hint of rain.

## ~ *The Hot Spot* ~

Sanctuary Wood
Tuesday, 4th May

We stumbled on a hot spot near St Jean, wounded were trailing by, dragging one leg after the other, horses were lying at the roadside dead and dying and everything was at a fever point. A cottage I called at, still inhabited by the peasants, helped us none but in the end, tired and shoulders aching, we got to Sanctuary Wood.

Yesterday, Monday, while Tuley and I were making stew for the lads who were digging, we got the order again to trek. After almost falling asleep in the trenches, we fell in, marched along the Zonnebeke road, then toddled home again to the wood itself this time, as the dug-outs are abandoned pending the retiral. After a fair night's sleep, Bill Swan and I had a feed of 'Maconachie'* and a drink of tea. I found the 'Maconachie' yesterday in a bag labelled 'Anti-Aircraft'; it was fired all night.

This morning is mild after raining all night; we're working in a new dug-out for tonight as the shells are coming over in style.

## ~ The Listening Post ~

Sanctuary Wood
Thursday, 6th May

On Tuesday night we, A & B Companies, relieved the 1st Argylls. The trenches have been hastily constructed about 400 yards behind the previous line and have only been occupied about a couple of days. The parapet is yielding, is very low and the water is knee-deep in parts owing to the ground being boggy and the weather showery. The trench is on the outskirts of a wood, the Germans are following up about 500 yards away in the open, just on a ridge, Hill 60 is just on our right.

I was on the listening post with Lance Corporal Watson and Sellars on Tuesday night, but the Lieutenant was more enterprising than the Lance Corporal, he took Watson and I last night to 100 yards or so from the German lines. We crawled through the bushes cautiously, hiding from star shells till we got into the open where we lay dead quiet listening for some time. We heard them signalling on a kind of wheezer which was repeated down their line and their picks were rattling. Evidently the ground was nice and rocky for them.

We move about the wood at the rear of the trench freely, digging and running for water any old time we please. Shells have been coming over but the spell has been pretty comfortable on the whole,

---

* Tinned stew with vegetables; it made a very pleasant change from bully beef.

though a lot of work has been expected off very little grub. We are getting relieved tonight but I am looking forward to a little excitement on the listening post before we go. There is always the chance of meeting each other when we'd rather not.

## ~ *A Fierce Artillery Duel* ~

Sanctuary Wood
Saturday, 8th May

We were relieved on Thursday night and have spent the time since then in the wood behind the trenches bordering on an open heathery patch. We each have a dug-out for ourselves as a precaution in the event of shelling and I made mine fragrant with pine flooring and roofing, the bushy shoots make a cushy bed.

The weather has been brilliant. A fierce artillery duel has been raging all day.[55] We had our innings in the morning but the Germans poured the shells all the afternoon into the clump on our left searching for our guns. We had splinters flying about us but no one was seriously hurt. 'Jiny' had a shake up with a splinter but is all right again. A Lieutenant and two men are lying in heather in front here, killed this morning in the trenches.

## ~ *Incessant Shelling* ~

Sanctuary Wood
Monday, 10th May

More shelling yesterday and a 'Stand To' in support to the 'Glosters'. Sellars and I had to wait in a dug-out on orders and we had a pleasant chat and a glorious tuck-in with Lieutenant Robb who had just returned from hospital and brought a delicious gingerbread cake with him. We made oxo and tea on a little 'Pocket Primer' he carries. He told us of a renegade Englishman caught spying and of a mysterious German gun within our lines which shells Poperinghe nightly. Lieutenant Stewart told us of a splendid advance made near Arras and a French advance on our left. The effect of such news on our fellows dead beat and hungry makes them giants again for endurance. Our little lot were relieved in the early morning but the shelling has hardly abated.

I'm writing these notes while we're 'Standing To' again. The Germans are kicking up an unholy row – the whole ground about us is shuddering. Lance Corporal Hamilton and Sergeant Thompson have just been hit by bullets, not mortally I think. Sometime I'll open these pages for the last time perhaps. One never knows. I pray the Lord who died of His love for us to pity our foolishness, my foolishness and in the last, to give us the certainty of meeting our loved ones when the day breaks on a New World.

Today is boiling hot. Sellars and I accompanied Lieutenant Stewart to locate a trench line in our rear. He told us that we were to hold this line[56] and cover the retiral of our Brigade should this be deemed necessary. This is no small compliment to our Battalion.

I received letters this morning from Carrie and Alec Mitchell.

## ~ *'Qui Vive'* ~

Sanctuary Wood
Wednesday, 12th May

In the trenches again. Came in on Monday night, occupying the same traverse as on Tuesday to Thursday last, only more exciting, constantly on the 'qui vive'. Poor Jimmy Smith killed yesterday in neighbouring traverse, on the eve of his discharge, the circumstances are particularly sad. Wrote Carrie yesterday. Just started shelling our trenches so story will be continued later.[57]

## ~ *Dreaming of Food* ~

Sanctuary Wood
Friday, 14th May

Poured all yesterday and today. I guess we're both [*British and Germans*] pretty miserable, they've been pretty quiet over the way. Nothing doing on the 'Listening Post' last night. Received letter from Carrie this morning. Had beautiful dreams of hot bannocks* buttered and eggs; could about smell them for hours after. Write and ask what the book says about this.

## ~ *Cheerful Resignation* ~

Sanctuary Wood
Monday, 17th May

Relieved from the fire trench on Saturday night and occupied the support trench 100 yards in the rear. I roofed a part over and made it more comfortable. Sunday was bright and quiet on the whole till last night when some hot work was doing on the Menin Road.

Today is raining. Reduced to a state of cheerful resignation to anything that may happen. The air is heavy with good rumours, big advance, long rest and a possible trip home.[58]

## ~ *A Dry Day At Last* ~

Sanctuary Wood
Thursday, 20th May

Still lying in the wood waiting for the relief that is always coming 'tomorrow'. We're buoyed up with the prospect of furlough as in

---

* Scottish delicacy, being a type of chewy oatmeal cookie.

truth we needed buoying up with the drenching rains these last few days. Today is the first dry day and it has been splendid. Things have been quiet as far as big fighting goes but there is a steady dribble of casualties.

Received a parcel this morning from Bella; temperature went up to fever point. Just heard another official wire that Italy has sailed in. Sounds probable this time in view of Tuesday's news in the 'Daily Chronicle', if right, well – the Huns, God pity them!

## ~ *Kind Remembrances* ~

Sanctuary Wood
Saturday, 22nd May

Yesterday was quiet, weather very fine. Today is still bright but a shadow is over our spirits as poor Bill Whitlie has just been carried away dead, shot through the head. We're preparing to leave the trenches tonight, 'redding up'.*

Received a 'Round Robin' from Mr Sponder this morning. I appreciate very much the kind remembrances of the old school. 'Tis a pity our ways must always be separate but will accept each other's good wishes and be happy. Our ways may meet the other side of the valley when we see the Promised Land spread before us.

## ~ *Sodom and Gomorrah* ~

Busseboom
Tuesday, 25th May

To pick up the broken thread and continue spinning the tale, here goes. On Saturday night we left our trenches to the care of the King's

---

* Slang for tidying up, a joyous event in the trenches and reminiscent for many young lads of the end of a school term and the accompanying revelries.

Own Yorkshire L.I. and moved off through the wood by platoons, the rendezvous being the level crossing near Vlamertinghe. Before we left the wood a burst of rapid fire ripped through the trees and accounted for a few, our Corporal was hit in the groin.

Beyond the range of rifles, passing along Zillebeke along the Menin Road into Ypres, we saw the hideous ruins, the result of the last bombardment. Words haven't been coined to describe the desolation. The brimstone rained on Sodom and Gomorrah could hardly have caused more havoc.

We reached the crossing, the road a living line of troops trekking backwards. Motor buses which not long ago picked up the gents and mesdames in the Strand, here picked up the fellows who were very exhausted, while the rest of us made for a field nearby where our field kitchens supplied us with hot tea, bread and butter after our packs had been loaded on limbers. With easy backs, well packed innards and light hearts, we started off again.

The beauty of the countryside got through the sweat over our eyes but we were utterly done, blistered feet chiefly, before we covered the 10 miles or more, being on the road from 10 p.m. on Saturday night to 5 a.m. Sunday morning. The camp was in a grass field between Reninghelst and Poperinghe, a bivouac being made with cabers and blankets.

Sunday the 23rd, three months since we left Edinburgh, was a tropical day. Our chief concern was to defend ourselves from the hot glare of the sun. After strategising by plunging about in a cold bath, I retired to the shelter of the bivouac. But I've forgotten – our parcels. What a deluge of cake, chocolate and the hundred other things that go to make parcels! I had my share from Bella, Carrie and Jessie Mathieson.

Later a few of us adjourned to an éstaminet nearby where we had coffee and a singsong. It was a welcome sight to see the kiddies, especially one little laughing curly-haired elf. I don't know whether it was a boy or a girl but it bubbled over with fun when we played peep-bo.

That night we slept soundly; the air was warm and heavy but at

5.30 in the morning following the steady booming of cannon overnight brought its sequel – a 'Stand To'. Our hearts beat slower at this – our 'rest' over before it was begun.

It is 8.30, the moon is sailing in a pale blue sky, let's lay down till tomorrow.

## ~ Gas Attacks ~

Busseboom
Wednesday, 26th May

We waited all Monday in a state of tension. We could smell the gas and the wind was blowing strongly against us but not until 5.30 p.m. did we move off. On the road back, about 200 dropped out from footsoreness principally, though the heat was terribly oppressive on us with our greatcoats and heavy packs. We lay in a field all night near some batteries not far from the rendezvous of Saturday night. We heard that massed attacks helped by gas were made near Menin Road, that the trenches we occupied had been lost and recaptured and that the Germans were concentrating strongly. We, however, it seemed had re-established all lost ground with some additional trenches.[59]

After lying in reserve with the rest of the Brigade until 10 a.m. on Tuesday morning we got sudden orders to move off again, but this time to huts behind Vlamertinghe where we had tea and found shelter from the heat. The crisis appeared to be over and at 3 p.m. a column of buses drew up and we had a welcome drive back.

I should note that some half-dozen of our officers are on leave in England for some days so we are without Colonel or Adjutant and if a show had come off for us, our Battalion would have been in the charge of our Company C.O. We are camping in a clump of trees and briars north of the last bivouac near Poperinghe. The nearest village is called Bosselboom or 'something'. The heat is terrific and we move about dressed like classical dancers.

Last night we got the week's mails that were lost during the St

Julien shoot-up. I got one from Bella, Carrie, Father and a packet of choc and a letter from Jessie Mathieson. Today General Snow visited us. The heat has been scorching but a delicious breeze is now stirring through the trees. We have just returned from an incident of the first importance – our bath – a clean skin has never been more appreciated. The bathtubs are in a quondam [*former*] school in Poperinghe. The water had seen previous service but it was hot and soapy.

The town has a deserted appearance owing to the shells that the Germans managed to throw into it, but quite a number of firm-lipped women were gleaning* in the fields and training the hops. The town is a mixture of rambling houses and handsome buildings, quite a nice place to spend a day in, but c'est impossible.

### ~ *Popular Songs* ~

Armentières
Sunday, 30th May

The past few days we've led a tinker's life. We bade adieu to Bossenboom on Friday morning at 4.30 a.m. marching to Dranoutre swinging along to 'Hold Your Hand Out', 'Persian Rose' and 'Row, Row, Row', in fact all the popular favourites on the brass bands of the 'Sherwood Foresters' and the 'Lincolns'. On Saturday morning we marched to Steenwerck. This afternoon we started off after dinner, reaching Armentieres about 8 p.m.

### ~ *A Talented Barber* ~

Armentières
Monday, 31st May

Another splendid day. Little groups are strolling about the square in

---

* Gathering the useful remnants of a crop from the field after harvest.

the sunshine. I was too tired last night to mention all the details which kept up the interest on the march.

On Friday afternoon Lance Corporal Watson and I got a pass into the village of Dranoutre. The barber was a fair English speaker and carried on the éstaminet and shoemaker's business along with his tonsorial activities.

In the evening we had a regular band performance in the 1st Royals' billets. All the old Prince's Street Gardens selections, just like being at home, lying on the grass and joining in the chorus. We bivouacked in the open that night.

June 1915

*The battalion was allowed a well-deserved week's rest at the start of the month, after which it manned trenches at Chapelle d'Armentières to the south of Ypres. Although still on the front line, casualties were mercifully light – just one killed, one wounded and two missing.*

~ *The Kilt Everywhere* ~

Armentières
Tuesday, 1st June

On Saturday I got into the village of Steenwerck which is the local transport centre. I had a tuck-in in an éstaminet where I met Budlock the quondam runner now a motor transport driver, one of the army aristocrats. Here also I got off Carrie's parcel in the 9th Divisional Post Office.

On Sunday we had a Service in the field after which the Colonel read to us congratulatory messages from Generals Joffre and French and divisional generals for the part we played in the rumpus of 22nd April and following days. Owing to the Colonel commanding the Composite Brigade being killed, the work of the different units was unknown.

After dinner we marched off through Steenwerck and other villages to Armentieres. Here Kitchener's Army[60] is in force, all Scottish units, the kilt everywhere, Gordon tartan, Cameron and Seaforths. The 9th Division drove the Germans beyond the town at the point of the bayonet last September and the line has been stationary ever since. In the interval both sides have fortified the positions and neither side attempts an offensive, so here we come for a rest. Occasionally a few shells are dropped in the town.

Our billet is the Civil Hospice, a clean, roomy building on three sides of the square. The place has been bathed in sunshine since we came and the square is ideal for a parade ground.

Yesterday, Monday, I ferretted out the 8th Gordons' billets and Alick Mitchell; he looks bronzed and brawny.

Today, Tuesday, we've finished a stiff morning's drill and bayonet work on the square in the sweltering heat. As the reports put it, 'I must put on record' the splendid time we've been having lately, the life is as perfect as one could look for 'here below'. Nobody could be anything else but happy – the destruction of the Huns would complete it.

Armentières
Monday, 7th June

Misc.

~ *'Estaminet de la Lique'* ~

Chapelle d'Armentières
Wednesday, 9th June[61]

I've been so busy doing nothing up till now that I'll require to paint the wasted days with the Irwin Cobb touch[62], leaving out the 'revolting details'.

Well then – Tuesday – Alick Mitchell – that is the first instant. Then the bath at the laundry, huge tubs of warm soapy suds, waist high, a cold plunge and a change. Route march in the sweltering heat.

Met an old Gorgi tough*, a lance jack in the R of Ks [*King's Royal Scots*] crush, something Royal Scots. Saturday, perhaps – éstaminet de la Lique, Rue de Flanders then 'Claude', dark and handsome, jovish beauty. Refugee d'Ypres if you like to believe her. Leicester Square accent surer than her Flemish. Very 'droll' in the French sense. Monday and Tuesday – swimming in the Lys, great sport.[63]

Last night part of the Battalion relieved the 1st A.&S.H. part of No. 8 Platoon in reserve trench. Walked in and hung up our equipments as casually as we would hang up our coats in the lobby at home.

Today, fine as usual, monotonous and dragging. Not a shot, one or two shells sent across to give the Germans something to do tonight in the way of rebuilding. Trenches the last word in comfort, surroundings almost the last word for beauty: the high road, the railway, the ruined farmhouse. 'The American' by Henry James.

## ~ *"Good Morning, Scotsmen"* ~

Chapelle d'Armentières
Monday, 14th June

Still in the trenches, the day opens at 'Stand To' at 1.45 a.m. with the Germans shouting across 'Good morning, Scotsmen', 'Cuckoo' and encoring our bursts of rapid fire. The rest of the day is spent dozing and reading in the sunshine or listening to piano.

One K.R. [*King's Royal Rifle Corps*] Rifleman gave a bright recital yesterday, entertaining us and the Huns across the way to all the Pantomime favourites, rippling waltzes, etc. Had a fine spread with Lance Corporal Watson from the officer's servants at Headquarters yesterday. The Colonel's cook produced a second course of custard, stewed rhubarb and milk – trés bon. Rumours circulating about guides having the preference in the granting of a week's furlough to Edinburgh – I'll wait and see. Things look rosier already at the prospect.

---

* One who hails from 'a lively area' of Edinburgh.

### ~ *A German Soldier's Grave* ~

Chapelle d'Armentières
Thursday, 17th June

Relieved from the reserve trenches on Monday night, we came back about half a mile to lie in support. We are bivouacked in the garden of what has once been a pretty suburban establishment: stables, shuttle alley, tennis court and orchard full of cherry, apple and pear trees and berry bushes. Our heads at night lie against the grave of 'A German Soldier', a pencil note on the back of the wooden cross says, Died of nine wounds May 1915. German sniper more likely, it's easy to guess how he got his wounds.

On Tuesday night a patrol of C Company, a Lieutenant and two men, were scouting in front of the German entanglements. They were caught between a German working party and their patrol – one fellow got back, the others believed to be prisoners.

Spend the days pleasantly in a jumped-up éstaminet – a private house really – the staff: Marie, two married sisters, Helene and Blanche. Helene favoured us with a French love song last night (after we came back from a forward patrol to the trenches). Except for this little place, La Chapelle d'Armentieres is pretty dull, and dully pretty.

### ~ *Chez Lepan* ~

Chapelle d'Armentières
Monday, 21st June

Since I last wrote I've discovered another howff [*meeting place*] in the farmhouse of a M. Lepan. He has one son and three daughters on the farm: Auguste, Clemence, Sophie and Marguerite aged 10½. Sophie and Marguerite are particularly good looking. An easy good humour is over the whole place and I've spent a good few pleasant hours in it.

Helene's establishment is brighter just now; Blanche's brother has been invalided home from the war, wounded at Rheims and fever followed. Pantry aprons and transparent blouses are worn in his honour.

## ~ *Promotion to Lance Corporal* ~

Chapelle d'Armentières
Sunday, 27th June

In the firing line from Tuesday afternoon until Friday afternoon then back to La Chapelle d'Armentieres. Promotion to Lance Corporal in orders of 24th instant. Whiff of Ypres on Saturday morning, a few shells peppering the houses in the vicinity of Chez Helene Lemaine which took their mind off the cooking for a wee while. Tonight we go back to our billets in Armentieres.

Apropos to a paragraph in yesterday's 'Le Matin'[64] which I saw today in Sophie Lepan's, we heard the Huns shouting and singing opposite us on Thursday evening over the fall of Lemberg. Sophie's cousin Henri has a deal of information about Lille and the Germans – this will remind me to put it on paper when I have a little more time.

## ~ *Back in Armentières* ~

Armentières
Monday, 28th June

Back in Armentieres, billeted in the classrooms of a commandeered school. I must own to some regret at leaving La Chapelle; there was a warm friendship between us and the folks of the village that is impossible in town. It is no small thing to enjoy the friendship of the home circle of Chez Lepan for even three weeks. They reveal a much more wholesome side of the French character than is usually presented.

Returning to the items of interest that Henri, Sophie's cousin, told me yesterday; extracts from a letter from his parents which they got through by some means which weren't divulged and I didn't ask. They are still on the farm near Lille and after detailing the number of horses, cows, hens, etc., which have been 'bought' with paper money, they say the farm is now almost denuded of its livestock and their fortune is gone. The German artillery is ploughing and sowing the land with grain seed. Last season's harvest has been lifted by them, the Germans, converting the best bread to their own use and leaving the coarser grain bread and maize flour to the owners and the people.

Lille itself is strongly fortified with light artillery and mitrailleuses and 12 lines of trenches between the town and the present German fire trench. All the valuables and pictures from the four museums in the town have been removed to Germany. Their trenches are well and cunningly constructed for their purpose, their loopholes are about halfway up the parapet, the men have to kneel to fire. The trenches are thinly held, no doubt they reckon on their undoubtedly strong mechanical arm to balance this deficiency should a surprise attack be made. Lastly the German soldiers are heartily tired but the officers hold their heads high and freely brandish their revolvers at the slightest evidence of irritation at the cast-iron discipline. This is the sort of thing that is going to help us when we've knocked the feet from the Prussian bully-caste.

~ *Animal Ecstasies* ~

Armentières
Wednesday, 30th June

Still resting, weather showery but none the worse for that. Just returned from the baths; we're never so near [*to heaven*] how and as when we get into a hot bath. Plenty of soap and a change into clean shirts. Civilization with its daily bath at hand and fresh underclothes for the asking knows nothing of our animal ecstasies.

July 1915

*A relatively quiet month, still manning front-line and reserve trenches near Armentières; two members of the 9th Royal Scots were killed and three wounded.*

~ *'Poppy View'* ~

Armentières
Wednesday, 6th July

Relieved C & D Companies on Saturday night, myself and five men being allotted to traverse Line 17. This part of the line is a little in advance of the line on the left. The salient enables an enfilade fire being gained along the trenches on our left. This corner comes in for some attention from the artillery. A number of shells of small calibre were landed yesterday, but no casualties.

The enemy trenches opposite are over 500 yards away separated by a field of wheat sprinkled with patches of red poppies: this has given the name 'Poppy View' to one of the bays. Another bay is the 'Debating Club', the subjects for tonight being 'What Is Love?' and 'The Care of the Young'. Then we have the 'Ousel's [*Thrush*] Nest' with its hair parted in the middle and 'Rest and be Thankful', 'Bow Bridge', anything in fact you fancy. The trenches are equal to the best; they have to be kept clean to abate the fly nuisance which has come to the front these intensely hot days.

Time is dragging, the routine is as monotonous as a city office, the only diversions are an occasional 'flutter' or a 'nark' [*annoying diversion*]. Reading is a bad third unless it's something light.

## ~ *Another Close Shave* ~

Armentières
Saturday, 10th July

Returned from the trenches again last night and billeted in the same school. The trenches were deadly monotonous on the whole, except on Thursday when the Germans sent over a few light shells. One crashed into the roof of my dug-out but the corrugated iron saved me and the woodwork was soon repaired.

Today I received a long letter from C and the sun is strong already, the speckled blue sky promises well for the week's rest.

## ~ *Church Service* ~

Armentières
Monday, 12th July

Had Church Service yesterday. The Revd Mr Beveridge is one of the Old School and spoke sincerely and earnestly. He appealed for recruits for a body, similar to King Arthur's Knights of the Round Table, swearing ourselves to white chivalry and all the rest. These splendid addresses I fear act on us spiritually like the passing brilliance of a star shell.

Today I am on guard duty with three men in the billets here but we are getting relieved for a little to go with the Company to the baths, God be praised.

## ~ *Guard Duty* ~

Armentières
Tuesday, 13th July

We were at the baths yesterday again. After 'lights out' last night, being on guard, Lowe and I were free to have a walk through the

**'One feature of the place I've neglected to mention are the windmills set on every hill.'** Windmills were a familiar sight in the Belgian countryside; here, Dickebusch Mill, 1914.

**'The square is ideal for a parade ground.'** Armentières town hall and market square, November 1914.

**'Then you reach Brussels, losing only two junior officers and some two hundred men.'**
German infantry on the offensive in Belgium.

**'Everything was prepared for except the Belgian joggle.'** Belgian troops defending one of the
roads leading to Antwerp.

'**The Kaiser claims the alliance of God sincerely or insincerely.**' German soldiers with begarlanded busts of the Kaiser and von Hindenburg which they have carved.

'**I would do a long pilgrimage to lay flowers on the grave that holds your body.**' The grave of an unknown German soldier.

'The boxing was laughable while Jake was in the ring, Smith was in a class by himself, but Tommy Docherty fought clever and gentlemanly bouts.' A boxing tournament held by the London Scottish.

'The General has not the figure of the pattern soldier but is rather smallish . . . I cannot tell what nature is hidden by a pair of kindly beaming eyes and good humoured features.' Lieutenant General Pulteney (second from left) conversing with Guardsmen.

**'Aeros are flitting about like butterflies.'** A German aeroplane flying over Ypres.

**'We went up to Bois Grenier again . . . it was silent as the grave.'** 'No-man's-land', Bois Grenier, June 1915, with British lines marked 'O' and German lines 'X'.

'The weather is becoming more unsettled, driving rains and cold, but so long as we are here we can laugh at it.' 9th Royal Scots marching in wet weather, September 1916.

'Alick, dear, dear Alick, staunch and true, generous, open as the day. I loved you as a brother and would gladly have given myself in your place. Never will I meet your like again, never will I forget you, never will I mourn you as I ought.'

'Leaving tonight on a week's leave, so the narrative must be brought up-to-date at the gallop.'

Beatson's final journey home involved him travelling by train to Boulogne, catching the ferry to Folkestone and the train to Victoria station, London, shown here, before continuing on to Edinburgh.

**'Sometime I'll open these pages for the last time perhaps. One never knows.'** All that remained of High Wood, the scene of Beatson's death, after its capture by the British.

**'I pray the Lord who died of His love for us to pity our foolishness, my foolishness and in the last, to give us the certainty of meeting our loved ones when the day breaks on a New World.'** High Wood today – the arrow marks the approximate spot in the cornfield where Beatson was killed.

streets. Not a light is visible except what filters through chinks in the doors and shutters. We came back to the school and opened the door of the concierge's apartment to find him and one of the Camerons struggling and cursing. We sat down after pouring oil on the troubled waters. The Cameron left and the concierge went upstairs with a candle saying 'Bon soir' to ourselves and jerking out a threat at a woman and her husband who were sitting looking on disinterestedly. The husband immediately stretched himself out on a sheet against the wall, half under the table and fell asleep and the woman told her story. We left at midnight.

Guard was dismissed this morning. I intend writing off some arrears while the Company is out on a route march.

## ~ *Deadly Monotony* ~

Armentières
Saturday, 17th July

Tuesday afternoon about 70 shells landed in the town, mostly of small calibre and only of local effect. Town Hall, a very old and historic building, was damaged, a few casualties. Our company was lodged in the cellars of a linen warehouse for an hour or so.

Wednesday, quiet again, afternoon very wet. Thursday night back to the trenches, weather very unsettled, deadly monotonous. Artillery sniping occasionally on both sides. Tonight we take over a trench on our right.

## ~ *Last Birthday* ~

Armentières
Tuesday, 27th July

Nothing of interest happened lately. Billeted in houses in Rue de Faubourg de Lille since we came out last Wednesday. Helene, Blanche and the others passed yesterday morning on their way to the train for St Omer. La Chapelle is emptied of its citizens and there is a steady stream of vehicles laden with furniture leaving the town here. Yesterday, too, was my first birthday spent on active service. I guess it won't be the last if I've any more to come.

August 1915

*From 3 to 16 August the battalion rested at Erquinghem; thereafter, it again manned the trenches and exchanged sporadic gunfire with the enemy, with one soldier being killed and three wounded.*

*It was during this month that Beatson, by now promoted to Lance Corporal, read in a magazine the diary of a dead Prussian soldier, named 'Heinrich', and wrote extensively of his 'conversation' with him.*

~ *Fire Fight* ~

Armentières<br>Monday, 2nd August

We came up to the trenches here, opposite Rue du Bois village, last Tuesday night. The trenches dart to and from each other, sometimes 400 yards or more, sometimes less than 70. At one part of the line a few hundred yards along to our right, the trenches are about 65 yards apart; closer contact is gained by sapping from each trench to within 30 yards distance which provides opportunities for bombing. Opposite us and a little half-right, the German trench runs along the main gable of a house in the cellar of which the soldiers lived during the day with only a lookout.

On Saturday night we made a feint to draw the Germans off the trench, at the same time punishing them heavily. At 6.15 p.m. three regiments, the Glosters, 9th Royal Scots and 1st Royal Scots opened a furious rapid fire, the machine guns rattling away in two-step time, ta-ra-rum-tum-tum. The artillery started mildly and we slackened our fire, stopping completely at 7.15 when our guns blazed forth a continual stream of shells. The large contact shells crashed through barbed wire entanglements and parapets, sending up columns of smoke and earth like volcanic eruptions. The house referred to was gouged out to its foundations and anything left alive was smothered by the shrapnel vomiting fire and bullets all along the line. This thundering row went on for an hour or so then stopped. The 'second house' started at 10 o'clock by which time we reckoned they would have got back their breath and started repairing the damage; more rapid firing, machine guns and shells, a fine row, splashes of fire all over them. I guess they got a jolly drenching before they found shelter.

On Sunday morning everything was quiet again, the sun shining brightly over the romantic countryside where the grey and khaki men contest their skill in brain and brawn. The khaki sons had the whip hand on Saturday night and showed it.

Tonight, Monday, we are being relieved by the P.P.C.L.I. [*Princess Patricia's Canadian Light Infantry*] and go back for a spell of hard labour, perhaps necessary, but it cuts to have it called 'rest'. The trenches are preferable by far in this weather.

Tuesday, 10th August
[*Date written but no entry made*][65]

~ *'Arms and The Man'* ~

Erquinghem
Wednesday, 11th August

We came back on Monday night of the 2nd instant, a fine moonlight night, star-spangled sky, but the eternal freshness of nature couldn't prevent us feeling dead beat when we reached our bivouacs. We can see troopers cantering by at all times along the path beside the canal. Yesterday a general rode past with a mounted escort carrying lances and pennons fluttering. Occasionally a barge with sails big-bellied with God's own breezes glides slowly by. The river is almost, if not quite, stagnant and looks more like a canal. Away across the flats the chimneys of Steenwerck are smoking. Just over the river by a pretty bridge is Erquinghem, hardly a country town like Armentieres but it has a few shops, éstaminets and an 'Hospice Civil'. At present it is the Red Cross Headquarters for this part of the line.

To come to more personal affairs, our huts are a bit overcrowded and it is too cold to sleep out without additional covering. The nights are frequently very sharp and heavy dews fall, but the day is usually hot. The work has been very heavy here for some days, up at 6.30, physical exercises 7.30 to 8.30, breakfast at 8.30 to 9, company drill 9.30 to 12.30, inspection or route march at 2.30. This timetable played havoc with our internal organs so for some days a band soothed our weary hearts at 3 p.m.

There is now a complete change of programme. Squads are working night and day on a blockhouse at Bois Grenier, about four miles from here. The night before last, when our squad was up, a battery nearby fired intermittently and we could see the shells shooting across the black background of sky and trees like white meteors. For all the time I've been out, this is the first time I've seen a shell en route.

I read an article this morning by Israel Fanquill on 'Arms and the Man'. It is brilliant and sincere, the product of an earnest, penetrating mind. The force of the latest 24 inch Austrian mortar, by an effort no greater than the picking up of a pin, uprooted a town eleven miles off with his first shot. The cataclysm evoked by a gunner utterly transcends his own muscles, perceptions or emotions. To dare serve a Krupp or Armstrong gun, one should be as tall as an Alp, as good as an angel, as wise as a god. A man lives up to the extreme height of his moral and physical nature when he dares to loose an arrow from the bowstring. It is true that men who loose titanic forces like a joke, coolly, are themselves broken down by an inferno similar to that of their own cold creation.[66] What wonder if, in such a hellish hurly-burly, the higher nerve centres are disintegrated and men revert to a primitive somnambulistic subconsciousness, deaf, dumb and blind. The stoutest soldiers break in madness, paralysis, convulsions, asphasia and delirium. I haven't seen much of that but he's on it when he says 'If we must needs quarrel among ourselves, return to fisticuffs'.

## ~ *The Calm Before The Storm* ~

Erquinghem
Thursday, 12th August

Yesterday afternoon we held battalion sports, good running and interesting boxing. One Farriermond, a sturdy little lad, won the mile and half mile races in fine style, he runs in much the same style as Kolehmainen.[67] Anderson of D Company won the sprint. The boxing was laughable while Jake was in the ring, Smith was in a class by himself, but Tommy Docherty fought clever and gentlemanly bouts. I was sorry that aching muscles kept me out of the sport; it was a great success and I hope it won't be long before we have the same again.

After tea we went up to Bois Grenier again. I stepped into a village, it was silent as the grave though most of the houses are still standing. Only one or two Red Cross men were loafing around, it has been a sort of residential suburb to Armentieres. I think the houses were handsome, pretty lanes and gardens and superior to the usual villages. We returned early this morning, a mouth organ lightened the road. Speaking about music, Lieutenant Wardrop has had a musical box sent out and we have all the catchy airs and waltzes to charm the summer day. In a letter from Carrie today, she sent the words of a song. I'll need to try and find the tune; it's just the thing for an exile.

Everything is quiet around here, there is a lull all along the western front practically, the calm before the storm, let's hope, and when it breaks, may it uproot and annihilate everything German outside of Germany. The papers and politicians are full of hints of something starting, that's what is needed to galvanise the creeping paralysis out of the people; there is a danger of them resigning themselves to something less than the utter and complete defeat of the enemy.[68] The soldiers anyhow are out for no compromise. It's an insult to the chums who have fallen already if we fail to finish their work by our own sacrifice. 'Thy will be done.'

## ~ *On the Blockhouse* ~

Erquinghem
Friday, 13th August

On the blockhouse today again at Bois Grenier. In the daylight I had a better chance of getting an idea of the elaborate scheme and details. The whole area, however, could be swept of everything living by a salvo of artillery, but is impregnable to infantry attacks; a regiment could hold an army corps. On the way up the Germans were searching for one of our batteries and almost found us.

Splendid weather.

## ~ *General Pulteney* ~

Bois Grenier
Monday, 16th August

Today has been thunderous and sunshining periodically, every little while we're sent helter-skelter for shelter by a sudden plump. This morning the battalion was drawn up on the flats beside the river and inspected by General Pulteney. He didn't address us but asked the Colonel to convey his compliments to us on our good behaviour, no court martials, etc. Sort of patted our baby curls and called us good boys; of course if we stray from the straight path there's a big stick in the corner. The General has not the figure of the pattern soldier but is rather smallish, I should say about 5'6" or 5'7" with the student's stoop and round shoulders.

I cannot tell what nature is hidden by a pair of kindly beaming eyes and good humoured features.[69]

Our rest finished at 3 o'clock, as part of the battalion goes into the trenches tonight and our Company is lying in reserve. We are billeted in huts in a little field full of pear trees, part of a farm on the roadside. Ripe old farm buildings, mossy brick walls and thatched and tiled roofs.

# Part III:

# The Conversation

~ *An 'Inhuman Document'* ~

Bois Grenier
Saturday, 21st August

It's a miserable morning, drenching downpour. It's some consolation to think of it like the grey drizzles, drenching the long heather and the cattle gazing stupidly through the mist at the white cottage. Oh humanity enveloped in a red mist – will it never struggle through?

When I started this diary I intended addressing my remarks to the shade of my sweetheart, but I was led from the base narrative of events. Love and war are not fit to be mentioned together; love makes us friends with the world, war violates us. Only God understands us – but all this is diversion. I forbade myself any self-revelation or wearing my heart on my sleeve; this confession even is out of place.

We still lie in reserve here beside the old farm. Last night for a little I listened to the boys raising the roof with their songs. Three girls sang something about 'You have Alsace but not our hearts'.

I was on duty with the guard till the early morning and passed the time reading the diary of a Prussian officer published in a magazine. Here I found a man I could love. The editor called it an 'Inhuman Document'. In a note at the beginning we are told there is no clue as to the officer's real name or regiment, only the name Heinrich in the upper left hand corner of the first page, so Heinrich let it be. Though you fight for a hellish system and your revolver might have finished me, I respect you. On the 21st of July the Colonel had a heart to heart talk with you all and that night the whole army entrained for Berlin. You gloried in being a German and had a jest at the lists.

> Berlin, August 1st [*1914*]. This is a great day. All is now settled with Russia. I was burning all last night lest the whole of this might turn out an illusion, but the dream has come true. France first, then Russia, Berlin is singing. France has not one thing prepared. No boots for the men, no fortress ammunition, no guns – nothing. One pities her but it has to be.

You heard too that England was going to fight alongside you, but you doubted it. You were no cripple to need help and we wouldn't be of much use anyhow.

In the train on August 5th you were worried about an unpaid bill for 30 marks payable to Kauffman the tobacconist for cigars. You can't write much in this place or you would telegraph Abel, but you can curse 'England'. That is the last date in your diary. Some days later you are treading on each others' heels waiting for you don't know what; rumours of the Belgians giving trouble, but that is absurd. You hear the first guns you have heard in warfare; you say you would shoot yourself if by some chance an order were to come to you to right about face and go back to garrison duty without approaching and feeling and smelling this giant of whom you are afraid – war.

It is clear who 'England' is for but it doesn't matter. The war leaves room for mention of the little inn with the garden full of flowers, of two white butterflies chasing each other in front of a regiment, of a bird's dust bath and even of flies. It seems to you that we move in the middle of a great deaf blind world that does not care a 'knutzer' for us and our affairs.

War brings out the character like drink, but much more perfectly if less violently. Von M, the man with the truth, is irritable over trifles. Hausen is moody and nervous when he has time to think. The war is bringing out the rash of some disease of the soul. The army is really one of the grave professions, we ought all to dress in black, never smile, never dance and carry Bibles. We have to do with death much more than the church. You think, Heinrich, that there is a chilly respect from your comrades because you don't play cards. You never mixed very well with the others, her ghost is your one and only companion.

Later, the Belgians, of all people in the world, making all that noise; it is inconceivably irritating. You believe in Luck and remind her of the little pig Napoleon believed in. Luck, then, there is nothing so like God on earth as the Great General Staff[70] who dispose of everything and who weave us all into one pattern for one supreme purpose. Extraordinary to think that thirty years ago a lot of this great army were not in the world and all the rest were blowing tin trumpets and beating toy drums. Funny to think that all this great hubbub once had a mother who smacked it and wiped its nose. That it cried in the dark for fear of bugaboos and ran to its mother's knee once for safety. Assuredly woman's work in this world is not small, when it can produce results like these and foster them.

Then religion, you keep an open mind, 'God will give us victory', the catch word of the army, no doubt of the French too, and the Russians. Depression, another day, fever and heat, depressed about the whole business. A nation is indestructible, or part of it, conquered territory is a curse. Look at Poland – it was cut up into three pieces ages ago and the three pieces are still alive and wriggling and anxious to join together again. Then thousands of Germans will be ruined but Hausen says the war will make Germany the richest country in the world, that not only France but England will be crushed and made into little states and that there will be one country only, powerful on earth, Germany.

The sight of the first war wounded went through you, bruised your susceptibilities. O wonderful and intricate world and universe in which, if an atom of matter were destroyed, the whole would tumble to pieces. Who knows but that the great German Army has been held in delay by the damned Belgians so that Captain Von H. may be given an opportunity of studying his own soul? Which is the greater? The army, which is but an ephemeral grouping of forms called together for a purpose whose actions and reactions, however wide, must still be as ephemeral as the earth itself? Or the soul of Captain Von H. which may be immortal. Then you reach Brussels, losing only two junior officers and some two hundred men, but there has been a frightful delay.

And the sights. You have no hatred for the men you are fighting; in fact they are not there. You are fighting to drive back a veil hung before you by fate, to escape through a nightmare to the clear world beyond. Of course there are moments when the individual enemy absorbs you. Astonishing moments in battle when a man suddenly appears before you. A man you have never seen before yet who, in a flash, suddenly becomes everything to you. He is the man coming to kill you yet you do not hate him in the least. Yet you take in every detail of his face; remember the face of a boy of eighteen or so, white, with teeth exposed and haggard eyes, like a runner in the last stage of an exhausting race. His eyes were on you yet they seemed unseeing, though like a furious mechanical figure, he was about to pitchfork you aside with his bayonet when your revolver did for him. Then the great laughing face of a heavy man of the innkeeper type, jovial, yet seeming petrified, laughing yet a thousand leagues from laughter and when I trod over it to get beyond, laughing no doubt still. Observe how Heinrich's sole idea is to get beyond. Hate, pity, love, mercy have absolutely no place in the stress of battle. He is imbued with the idea of the blow, 'Smash through to victory regardless of life'. That idea survives the sight of the wounded.

Then you go on to explain how the Belgian joggle [*slight shuddering*] struck back through the whole army even to the General Staff. The unexpected knock disorganised the machinery, so exquisite and perfectly balanced and so intricate. The super-efficiency in fact produced an inefficiency that held you. The whole thing might be likened to a bottle of milk which would have poured out easily but for the Belgian joggle that made butter of the milk and so blocked the neck. You clotted. Everywhere mechanism and the advantages of mechanism and its terrible faults. The feeding alone of this host must be a work for the gods. You have to feed men, horses and guns and they can't wait for their food. When God ordained that man must eat at least twice a day, He had perhaps wars like this in view. He wished to stop war from growing beyond a certain size. Vegetables and flowers cannot grow beyond a certain size, on account of the fact that their nutriment has to reach them through a single stem. An army of course may have many stems for its nutriment, but if it is condemned to feed through too few it suffers in consequence.

Then you decide that the soldier has no right to be philosopher when in the field. His philosophy ought to be left behind him like any other encumbrance. His brains should be used to the utmost on the military work before him. Then you say goodbye to Brussels and we meet in the early morning, hot hazy morning, beside new made graves but you are getting up to the enemy. The men are very fit, well and eager and the English are in front. Two days later, your regiment has been nearly decimated. Hausen is dead and Von M., also three other officers, others wounded, the colonel wounded, the men nearly annihilated. War, who grumbles at war? This is not war, it is the boldest and brutalest form of pig-headed butchery devised by fools for the destruction of German men.

. Then you curse the fools and yourself but resign yourself to Fate, which is the Army and Discipline. Were it not that you drive yourself with them, you would kill yourself for your crime. This is the greatest crime in history. They know it is impossible to advance in the old method under modern conditions and yet they make you. Result – Death. The enemy is behind you, Heinrich.

Later, close on Paris, dead from marching and starved, the taste of fever in your mouth. The enemy always in front of you like a cloud you cannot seize, a cloud that spits fire at you. Well are they dead, you reckon, those others.

A day's rest brings out all your weariness. The Belgian joggle still follows you. You are shaky from want of food and you have lost the little gold pig. You are heartbroken. You know it means you will never see her again. There are things that matter in this life more than death. Ah! The good Rhineland all in hot summer there and the men gone. They have been killed by a wrong military system. That is bad but forgivable. What is terrible and unforgivable is the fact that they have been killed by a wrong moral system, by men who say in their hearts of German men, 'They do not matter', of widows and fatherless children, 'They do not matter, crush them, kill them all so that we get our purpose'. You cry out against the arrogant place-men. You have hell in your heart beside starvation in your belly. Your spiritual agony makes you write things you would have been shot for if they were read. You would have been shot by the real enemy and so died a soldier's death.

I have spent a happy day with you, Heinrich, tomorrow will come none too soon. Good night.


## ~ *Heinrich's Soul* ~

Bois Grenier
Sunday, 22nd August

A hot summer morning, the weather that brings out butterflies and thoughts. It is good to remember such a morning as this in a past age, making for the open country with the little figure in cornflower blue. How happy then! How happy in a different way, reading and loving the soul of a dead Prussian officer. Heinrich would have loved such a morning as this – before the war. After – his soul was in an agony of shame, seeking for the reason and righteousness to clothe it.

The next entry in your diary. You are all moving back, yourself in the uniform of a dead Frenchman and in a trench. All you possess is your diary which you have because the French soldiers were gentlemen and took your word that it was private. The trenches were prepared years ago in case of a defeat in the attack on Paris; not cut actually but prepared for. Everything was prepared for except the Belgian joggle and that torments you still.

Germany is lost, she aimed not to be a nation but a mechanism and succeeded in her aim. All is a great darkness in which you see no light and yet you have come to know your own soul that had been lying dead in your mind or dreaming all these years. You see tremendous things, just as years ago when your imagination was lit with drink. The Kings and Captains and peoples of the past appeased, only now your vision is clear as though the mind or your youth had returned. The summer is over and the harvest is gathered and the winter is on you; an endless winter until you break into the human land of spring. Germany will not live again till the flowers are growing upon her grave.

Then you reckon a trench is a prison and think six days a long time. The deadlock grates on you, the filthy bread, the vermin. The wounded, if they scream too much, they are stamped on. You are black with dirt, you stink and you laugh. Never, you say, was there such a madhouse, such a hell, such a charnel*, such an 'abattoir' all mixed together.

A night attack on us failed, you lost a number of men and got a bullet clean through your left arm. Raining incessantly, nearly deaf with the continuous noise of guns and bursting shells and suffering from a skin irritation; to scratch oneself increases the irritation, not to scratch is torture. And so the battle goes on between will and inclination whilst the guns boom away, announcing the lesser battle between flesh and iron.

Then you feel the loneliness, no books, no music, no letters for you, though the post comes all right – a month old about – and picture postcards showing the 'English'[71] running away. You know the 'English' do not run away. Men get chocolate, cigarettes and so forth, you get nothing. And people write to people but you write to no one. Abel has written, you suppose, but it has gone astray. She has not written. It would have been safe enough; she need not have signed her

---

* A vault where corpses or bones are buried.

name. You guess she said to herself, 'In the confusion of war it is better not to write. My letter may fall into hands belonging to tongues that might talk.'

O! You do hate the cautious woman whose one thought is Reputation, just as you hate the miser whose one thought is gold. And you wrote her every day in your book and I wondered why you never posted your eternally long letter. You told her it was a letter that could only be posted if you fell. It will reach her secretly and in a way that will cause no trouble – or it will not reach her at all.

Later – still the incessant noise. Not being able to change your clothes depresses you; your dreams are either terrific or delightful, the last are the worst. You woke this morning with the rain drizzling on you, saying to yourself 'War is the Serpent since changing his skin'. The French artillery is terrific, pins you down just as the great Gulliver was pinned down by the little people of that island. Their shells are always there. What that man in high command told you is worth noting. Though you are absolutely checkmated, he is not gloomy, only philosophic.

> Every situation has its spirit. There is no use looking at events; fix your eyes on the spirit of which events are only the clothing. Germany cannot now win because she has lost. In all the circumstances, victory could only have come to us in one way, by explosion. Had we shattered France all would have been ours. We failed to explode.
>
> Russia will not conquer us, France will not conquer us. England will not conquer us, no more than rust conquers an imperfect shell lying in a ditch. The shell has been conquered because the fuse or charge failed. There is a good deal of the lottery in war. We drew a blank. Napoleon would very well have understood this position, but our upper men have not the imagination to see the spirit of the situation.
>
> Good God! Hindenburg hammers away. If he were attacking a china vase he would smash it, but he is hitting a punching ball

on a stalk that gives it a swing from the Urals to the sea, and our men are falling all the time.

What spoilt the spirit of the situation? I will tell you – our Politicians. They should have left England alone. England only wanted to sit still and be comfortable and now everyone is shouting against England. The shout began from our politicians who wished to cover up for the horrible mess they had made. England hates no one, she only loves herself. She was very friendly to us, very friendly. I know for I have spent much time there. She has a deep, profound and solid contempt for everyone but herself – that is her great fault but she is not ungenerous. She is a mob and very little in greatness of mind; she is not straight in internal politics, but she is straight in dealing with the States. She is the most curious paradox, very like a tradesman who is honourable in business but in his own house is unjust to his children. But to hate her is absurd and a waste of good energy. She did not fall on us as an assassin, she was dragged in by the asses who held our political cards.

O why was Bismarck not an immortal? We have no one. No one to play the game for us. Of which war is but the picking up of the stakes.

He went on:

The Kaiser is a true genius, a great, great man without the essential something that makes a great statesman. I think really it is a sense of humour together with plain commonsense that makes a really good nation leader. Bismarck had that sense of humour which illuminates as well as the commonsense that weighs. His short sentences were full of humour – even as a war-maker; compare him with that ass 'Bernhardi'.[72]

Your wound though slight gives you a good deal of pain. A man nearby had the toothache terribly bad all yesterday. You lanced his gum with a borrowed knife but it did not stop the pain. His head was blown off this morning. The men too, quite simple fellows, think the war has been too long prepared for. You know men who have been long, long preparing to be great and who die fameless. There is, you think, a spirit of these things that dies from being restrained. Military life long continued in peacetime kills the real military spirit. Self-assurance, arrogance, stiffness and brutal obedience to the cut and dried, kills the fighting spirit of a nation. Should the English make big armies of citizens they will be a terrible foe, and that is what you foresee. The Russians, too, have many of these terrible untrained men, and the French.

One night you have a singularly vivid dream of your mother, dead many years; your youngest brother was in the dream too. You have never dreamt of her, perhaps because she is always in your waking mind.

Then the end. You see an aeroplane shot down over our lines, fell like a bird shot suddenly dead. A remark that the food is a lot better lately. The commissariat is working better than it has for a long time. And the diary ends. Are you dead, Heinrich? I know you would die bravely and quietly. Fate has labelled you Prussian and me British, but I would do a long pilgrimage to lay flowers on the grave that holds your body.

It is a perfect Sunday afternoon. The blue sky is dappled with white puffs of shrapnel smoke; with that exception there is nothing of war. The suspense in Purgatory is a real terror if it resembles in any measure this eternal waiting, waiting.

# Part IV:

# Rumours and Rats

~ *Spiritualism* ~

Bois Grenier
Wednesday, 25th August

Sitting between the two walls of a trench, the hot day infuses informal activity into the insect life that pesters us: wasps, flies, beetles of all sizes and colours preying on us and each other.

Lately we have been discussing Spiritualism among ourselves.[73] Some are mystified and chary of the subject and claim to have seen manifestations of levitation and table rapping. I am open-minded on the subject; I have no timidity of it either. I pressed Boyd to try it with me which he did – without result; perhaps some special manner of approach or state of mind is necessary. It cannot be that there is any lack of spirits, German or British.

Our Company came in last night; the Germans are about 400 yards in front of us. They no doubt feed their patriotism with the news of the Russian retreat, while we feed ours on the splendid naval victory in the Baltic and the brilliant generalship at the Dardanelles.

There is at this moment absolutely no sound of conflict, indeed the artillery, only, keeps the play going. This morning the German guns peppered a trench on our left held by the 1st Royal Scots, to which our guns replied.

September 1915

*For the first two weeks of September the 9th Royal Scots were based at Bois Grenier and suffered three wounded in the German shelling of their trenches. The remainder of the month was spent at rest and the battalion travelled by train to Lamotte en Santerre for a period of training.*

## ~ *Rumours* ~

Bois Grenier
Tuesday, 14th September

Still lying in this calm backwater of the greatest war the world has known, but the rapids are not far ahead I guess from the signs. There is a rough journey and they are lucky who reach the broad sea with their bare life beating inside a bruised body.

The Germans opposite us are to be respected as fighters. Their snipers are busy and as the haze lifted the other morning we spotted a party working on their trench in full view of our lines. Our own sniper was wounded through his own foolishness through taking them too cheaply. Farquharson was shot dead the other night. My own opinion is that the fault lies with the officers who superintended the building of these trenches without carefully and abundantly loopholing them, and with the officers since then who have not troubled to correct the error.

It was intended that we should be relieved on Monday night, but the part of the brigade in the trenches stay on until tomorrow, Wednesday, night. What follows after this is conjectured, but all are excited over rumours of a train journey. Bangalore and St Omer are popular, Ypres, La Bassee or Arras have too ugly a look about them; mention them and you are a rank pessimist. But why all this sparring and nothing up our sleeves? That promises well for a grand slam. A Division, the 23rd, of Kitchener's Army takes over our part of the line.

Weather continues fine.

## ~ *An Early Start* ~

Vieux Berquin
Friday, 17th September

Spent yesterday at the camp near Erquinghem, loafing generally. Reveille this morning at 3.15 a.m. After cursing and scrambling in the dark for breakfast, the battalion marched off about 4.30, just as light was breaking. We reached Vieux Berquin about 9.30, some 17 kilometres distant. The men are fit and well as a whole; finished smartly and well within themselves. The village is apparently used as a motor transport department. It is a clean unpretentious place in pretty surroundings.

## ~ *General Pulteney's 'Adieu'* ~

Vieux Berquin
Saturday, 18th September

We were inspected – well hardly that – drawn up with the other units of our brigade this morning to receive the adieus of General Pulteney. The 1st Royals and Argylls were right of the line, Camerons, 9th Royals and Argylls in the centre and the Glosters on the left. The ceremonies were admirably carried out, even to the regulation 'three times three'[74], all going like a machine. The General thanked us for our services while in his corps and wished us 'good luck and good fortune' at the part of the line we take over from the French. So that's the end of the rumours.

Later our Colonel complimented us on the march discipline yesterday and encouraged us to brace ourselves for much hard work shortly. The sun is hot and bright today, so nobody worries about the future.

## ~ *The Chapel at Vieux Berquin* ~

Vieux Berquin
Sunday, 19th September

The village was bright this morning, under a clear blue sky. Inside, the chapel was filled with pretty girls, chicly dressed, and widows, young and old, draped in black, with a sprinkling of boys and elderly men and soldiers, French, Belgian and British. The chapel is dead white inside, the altar of gold and white and pink, the confession boxes of carved woodwork with little pinnacles. A shell hole in the front is the only relic of the tide that receded from the village last October. The service was half in Flemish and half in French, conducted by a vivacious young fellow. An old woman hobbled among the congregation seeking charity for the Belgian refugees of the village. Madeleine Bagaert of Maubeuge is an exceptional specimen of the refugee species in this village.

We have finished tea and are packing up – move off tomorrow morning at 1 a.m.

## ~ *'A Hungry Village'* ~

Lamotte en Santerre
Monday, 27th September

A seven mile march in the dark, the twinkling lights in the distance, the screaming of the train whistles over the level crossings into the grimy little town of Hazebrouck, a hurried meal and into the trucks as the light was breaking.

Travelled all day, now fast, now slow, pounding through Amiens and drawing up in the late afternoon of Monday, the 20th, at Guillacourt. From there we marched with pipes skirling through Bayonvillers to Lamotte, in Santerre, six miles or so distant. French soldiers who had been already relieved crowded out from farm buildings and barns. I expect this is the first time British troops have been in the district since the retreat at the beginning of the war.[75]

We bivouacked in the gardens for a day or two before we moved into the farm buildings. The weather has been showery lately. The countryside is broad and flat, sparsely wooded; straight, easy roads with clusters of houses dotted over the plains, the spire of a chapel shooting up from each – the real provincial France. The types of the villagers are: the men, gaunt, grey-haired with straggling moustache, dirty shirt sleeves, slack pants and red waistband, a sort of broken-down brigand; the women, heavy, clumsy, agricultural, and nearly all in the way of increasing the family. We have to try and forget their dirt and live down their suspicions for the sake of the Entente Cordiale. This Lamotte is a hungry village. It is a year now since the Huns were here and it hasn't got its breath back yet. I have only seen one handsome woman in it, a well proportioned creature, a flower on a midden [*refuse heap*].

Battalions of French infantry passed us on their way back last Tuesday. The men were of a standard higher than the usual of the French but the march discipline was atrocious. Even with the trumpets blaring and bands playing, they shuffled along any old way.

A feature of the countryside are the wayside shrines; an iron filigreed cross high on a stone base, with a suspended figure of the Christ, sheltered from sun and storm by an arbour of trees.

Spies are said to be moving about, we had a 'suspect' the other night. There are some oddities no doubt; a Russian artist, long-haired and fat, a Keystone mob* with breeches, open-necked shirts and broad felt hats reminiscent of a haymakers' chorus in a comic play. Everybody is to be treated with cold distrust for the sake of the Entente Cordiale. I remember how Zola in the 'Sin of Abbé Mouret'[76] despised this breed of humanity peculiar to agricultural France. Heinrich, in his Prussian arrogance no doubt, would reckon them better dead. Only the soil they are wed to is responsive to their efforts and they live long and are happy.

October 1915

*The battalion was mostly at rest this month and undertook training exercises away from the front line; there were no casualties.*

## ~ *Marching to Chuignes* ~

Chuignes
Tuesday, 5th October

There is no doubt that France in the sunshine is a pleasure ground for the senses. There is passion in the bunch of rosy roofs that snuggle against the green slopes, in the sombre shadows that sweep across hills and hollows and are lost in the deluge of sunlight on the horizon.

---

* Presumably a reference to local gendarmes.

We marched from Lamotte en Santerre yesterday to Chuignes, ten miles or so winding through the valleys behind a rampart of low hills. The straighter roads over the hills are forbidden as they show against the skyline to the Bosches. The River Somme is seen here and there gliding over the plain, wheeling among the long grass or creeping through melancholy shadows; beyond it the fair country lay smiling to the sun. Oxen pull the ploughs and shrines abound where the mortal, who has been seduced by nature, may plead. I suppose where sinning is easy, the Church had to save them by some system not too troublesome. In a country where opportunities are less frequent, they can afford to put on the screw a bit tighter.

Chuignes has been in the arena twice. In the little graveyard in a common grave lies 'One brave Frenchman and seven brave Germans', in another, seventy-four French soldiers; here and there are the little mounds covering the bones of the fellows who fought among the houses. The chapel is always open, in fact a lookout is kept from the belfry. The processional banners still hang from the walls, two broken-winded harmoniums, the box pews, the altar, the plaques of the 'stations' all complete; the bell that used to call the faithful who now sleep now clangs the aeroplane alarm.

Our Company lodge in an old 'écurie' where the Frenchmen before us have erected hammocks with branches and wire netting.

## ~ The Scene Around Chuignes ~

Chuignes
Sunday, 10th October

I'll fill in the time scribbling before going on a working patrol up to the trenches tonight. To the east of the village there is a huddle of low hills and ridges with close woods and steep roads. The enemy have been driven from the first ramparts and are now hanging on to the crest of a hill beyond. We are a trifle higher than the Huns who are at some parts five yards off, at others 30, 50, up to 200 yards. The hill is of a limestone formation, honeycombed with mines. Explosions are frequent, a 'windy' bit of the line. Last night the Germans were caught taking down their barbed wire entanglements.

## ~ *Dead Bodies and Rats* ~

Chuignes
Tuesday, 12th October

The alarm spread through the whole brigade and there was a hurried 'Stand to Arms'. After an hour or two the coast was still clear and we peeled off our war gear and got down to it again.

On the outskirts of Chuignes the ground is full of dead bodies and rats. Little solitary graves with a wooden cross to 'Un brave soldat Allemand'. A Frenchman and a German lie alone vis-à-vis, face to face in a little hollow. In one grave lie 77 French soldiers, beside it 78 Germans in a grave about half the size. The place around is strewn with torn knapsacks, pouches and scraps of blue and grey cloth. A 'képi' on the French grave and tattered helmets lying about. The field mice have made a nest in a German mess-tin, crawling in and out through the rents a bullet has made. The fellows had some furious fun at nights baiting the rats. There is a plague of the repulsive vermin in the village; slow, fat, waddling monsters.

A party of us were up helping the French sappers the other night. The 'terrain' was a sort of sandy loam, easy to work yet the three 'genii' loafed and slept. The sap will be ready to charge when we are charging round about the Unter der Linden. That is if they don't get some encouragement in the way of something hard. The timbering was simple and strong. The sap I was on last night had not so elaborate a gallery owing to the enemy trench being so close, a low gallery for a few yards, a shaft down then a winding tunnel to beneath the German trench. This sap was almost ready for laying the charge. While I was turning the wheel that works the fan a German shouted across, 'How do you like your job tonight, Jock?' Unfortunately we have had orders to cut them dead when they become familiar.

We shifted yesterday and are lying in reserve in a group of buildings on the top of a hill. They are all loopholed and have got ill-used in the struggle for possession.

## ~ *More Rats* ~

Later

This is the place for the Pied Piper of Hamelin. Rats, rats, rats, ten per man at least and if you don't kill them you've got to feed them. They go into our haversacks and eat the biscuits, make free with our rations if we leave them exposed and scamper all over us when we try to sleep. They breed in the straw beneath us, around us and above us. Oh Stevenson, you would have been happy to live again in a daisy, what of a rat?[77] My God, to think these putrescent vermin were once laughing, moustached Frenchmen.

Alick, dear, dear Alick, staunch and true, generous, open as the day. I loved you as a brother and would gladly have given myself in your place. Never will I meet your like again, never will I forget you, never will I mourn you as I ought. May God count me worthy to meet you again, dear, dear brother of mine, Alick.*

Chuignes
Sunday, 17th October

Nothing doing.

## ~ *Action Without Motive* ~

Chuignes
Wednesday, 20th October

Still at the 'House on the Hill' doing fatigues, working the air fans at the sap heads and dumping the bags of earth. Not very heroic, is it? Still it is the part allotted to us. There are occasionally bouts of bombing but still very quiet and still the same ugly look about the situation. News is always coming along the line of progress and success in the Ypres, Loos and Champagne regions. Those fellows who fought on the Continent under

---

* Referring to the death of Sergeant Alexander Mitchell of the Gordon Highlanders, who is also mentioned on 10 May, 1 June and 9 June.

the Iron Duke or Sir John Moore[78] had the pull over us: they won habitable villages and substantial towns; they saw the symbols of what they fought for. Now we advance a quarter of a mile and capture a ditch, or three miles and gain a heap of ruins. Seems all action and no motive, n'est-ce pas? La vie est vaine, un peu d'amour, un peu du peine, et puis 'bon jour'.[79]

## ~ *Marching to Bougainville* ~

Bougainville
Thursday, 28th October

Since Sunday last we've been drenched and dried and padded the hoof for forty miles through a chain of villages with euphonious names – Saint Fuscien, Fluy, Floxicourt, Bougainville – as good as the New World's stars, Savannah or Silverado, second only to Caroline! We were relieved at Fontaine-les-Cappy on Sunday afternoon by French regiments from Le Souchez and Arras, matured warriors. It was dark and a drenching downpour by the time we reached Lamotte. We had two good nights' rest in the barn, paid a visit to Mme Valentine on Monday where we had chips and coffee and a tumbler of steaming red wine before we set off again on Tuesday morning. A raw, bitter morning it was too, till we were well on the road to Amiens.

Passing through Villers-Brettoneux and Boves, both fair sized villages, we reached the camp on the broad breast of rising ground above Boves, sheets of tents housing the entire brigade, some five thousand men. This camp was about five-and-a-half miles north of Amiens, twelve miles from Lamotte. The country around Amiens is a vast orchard, a garment of green with pearls of villages and streamers of lanes. We were denied entrance into the fair city itself so on Wednesday morning we set off along the lanes to the left of the city, through Saint Fuscien, Dury and Fluy. After some thirteen miles we halted at midday on the outskirts of Fluy for dinner, then another five miles through Pissy and Floxicourt to Bougainville; a pretty district, paradisaical almost – thick pine woods, mint scented fields and heavy laden apple trees skirting the road. The villages with the pond and shimmering reflection of the guardian chapel – but not a young man to be seen. Only a few fell out on the march. It is no mean task to do eighteen miles with a heavy pack and a straight back and grin and bear it, though I guess we could do a bit more without worrying about it.

November 1915

*Again, the battalion was mostly at rest and undertaking training exercises away from the front line; there were no casualties this month. The rest of the 27th Division was moved to Serbia but the 9th Royal Scots remained on the Western Front and transferred to the 5th Division.*

~ *Bougainville* ~

Bougainville
Wednesday, 3rd November

Still lying at Bougainville. The village is dull, a huddle of houses round the chapel and the grassy square or 'place' as they call it. There are only two cafés, 'de la Jeuneuse' and 'de la Place', worth the name, crowded every night for an hour. (There is another – 'des Mariees', dimly lit, with an upstairs.) The folk clearly regard us as a horde of thieves, with some justification from the scum of a sister battalion. Hitherto we have been able to correct the impression and make the Hunting Stewart tartan respected, but our latest drafts have little pride of honesty. The sale of cognac or rum is forbidden to all troops. The A.&S.H., indeed, are forbidden entrance to a café for the time being but the lighter wines are on sale from 11 to 1 and 6 to 8.

Our daily programme is rather lenient just now, route march or bomb instruction from 9.30 to 12.30 and free for the rest of the day practically, 'in billet' at 7, lights out at 9. The billet for No. 8 platoon is the loft of a farm building swept free from rats or mice and very comfortable. The weather is becoming more unsettled, driving rains and cold, but so long as we are here we can laugh at it. All the boys are enjoying themselves. On our route marches we have given the natives their first sight of the 'Kilties'. Molliens, Vidame, St Aubin-Montenoy and the other villages, all more or less deserted and decayed, everywhere the meagre male section is either in the bud or withered.

## ~ *More Rumours* ~

Bougainville
Friday, 5th November

The case of the 'Ninth' is becoming mysterious; it is impossible to deduce our fate from the mass of contradictory signs. On one side – all smoke helmets have been handed in, we've a cosy crib and no talk of the trenches. On the other – tonight we had cardigans issued, waterproof capes are coming and emergency rations are carefully inspected. On top of these facts is an army load of rumours. We're completely in the dark. Serbia would be an interesting change, that's as much as we can expect.

The war seems endless, we've come to regard it as a normal state of affairs. The mills of God grind so slowly and life is so short, loveless and colourless. The cheerfulness of the lads is amazing, they are never depressed for any length of time. Yet, why should we be? This is comparative luxury, some of our comrades thirty kilos off are shivering and counting the hours till dawn. When we have tasted the bitter we can appreciate the sweet, you bet.

## ~ *'God' is Bleeding* ~

Bougainville
Saturday, 6th November

From a German prisoner, after the Champagne drive: 'It was not a surprise attack?' asked the interviewer. 'No, we even learned the exact hour it was to take place.' I remember Heinrich said, 'There is nothing so like God on earth as the Great General Staff.'

From 'Vorwarts'[80] a Cologne incident, a bed and wardrobe were offered as a gift in a local paper. The applications were overwhelming. 'I am a poor soldier's wife, with two children, and have no bed – sleep upon the ground, my dwelling is open to inspection at any time.' Another, terribly pathetic: 'Have no wardrobe and as I am far gone in consumption, I need a bed to sleep alone. We have five children and four are dead.' Their 'God' is bleeding at the heart.

## ~ *The 27th Division goes to Serbia* ~

Bougainville
Thursday, 11th November

Yesterday the battalion was paraded and addressed by Brigadier General Croker. The brigade, except ourselves, goes east to Serbia while we, by all accounts, are to be attached to the 5th Division and remain in France. So rumours again have been put to death. He spoke very flatteringly of our services to the brigade and the 27th Division, while we honestly regret being left behind by our sister battalions, the Glosters, 1st Royals and Argylls.

The rainy season has set in, I guess, showers night and day.

## ~ *First Snow* ~

Bougainville
Tuesday, 16th November

Yesterday we saw our first snow this season and today the countryside is all grey and white. The monster winter has come smiling, everybody was bright on the march this morning. Some might not know why but I guess it was the snow, gently falling, and the broad sweep of white earth till it met the grey veil of sky.

We passed the Argylls this morning as they marched away. It seems quite matter of fact to see them with their bundle of necessaries, setting off to travel half the world over land and sea and carry on with the business. Our stay will not last much longer, I guess, since the brigade is moving.

## ~ *Before the Curtain Falls* ~

Bougainville
Sunday, 21st November

I've just read the last words of 'Paul Kelver'* and turned back to read the criticisms of the press. How feeble, I almost suspect them of prejudice. I number it among the books that will surely live. It has the germ of life in it, a plain man's Bible. I must see this man before the curtain falls, this Jerome K. Jerome, the interpreter of dreams of youth with his feet among the clay and his head in the clouds.

The weather is becoming chillier.

December 1915

*Stationed at Vaux throughout December, the battalion suffered two soldiers killed.*

*Beatson recorded his last entry before going on leave. Just over a week later, on the 16th, he married his sweetheart, Carrie, in Edinburgh.*

## ~ *Last Entry – About to Go on Leave* ~

Bois de Vaux
Tuesday, 7th December

Leaving tonight on a week's leave, so the narrative must be brought up-to-date at the gallop. We left Bougainville some days after the date of the last entry, marching by day and resting by night at the wayside villages of Ferrieres, Pont Noyelle, Sailly, Laurette and Suzanne. The second day's march took us through Amiens and gave us a glimpse of the Cathedral. That night we rested at Pont Noyelle looking up to the hills where a bloody skirmish was fought in the 70 war.†

At Suzanne, the advanced base for the line around here, we were impressed by the organisation and liveliness of the new division. A

---

* A semi-autobiographical work by Jerome K. Jerome published in 1902.
† The Franco-Prussian War of 1870.

picture house, a band, a regimental canteen, recreation rooms, every detail perfect. We had a Church service in the picture house Sunday before last, with the portraits of gay ladies and gallants gazing from the walls of the faded salle of the Chateau. Every few minutes a gun would roar, shaking the walls so that the crystals of the hanging candelabra tinkled musically. Next morning we relieved the 'Cheshires' in the battle dug-outs behind Vaux Bois. No water and lots of mud, so I was glad to link up with the new-formed scouts.

The situation here is a bit peculiar; the line is broken by the River Somme and its marshes, the space between the broken ends of the two lines.

\*     \*     \*

# Epilogue

## 'Khaki' Weddings

James Beatson married 'Carrie' Wight on 16 December 1915 at the Sheriff's Court House, Edinburgh. Their witnesses were Carrie's chief bridesmaid, Agnes Young Douglas, and Beatson's best man, John Alston, a civil engineer and presumably a work colleague from before the war. Beatson's diary records that he corresponded with both John Alston and a Miss Alston. Carrie's parents, Adrian and Margaret, were present, as was Beatson's father, John; sadly his mother had died before the war.

Beatson was, of course, not alone in taking the opportunity of leave from the trenches to get married. That same month the *Scotsman* reported on the 'remarkable increase' in marriages in Edinburgh. It has subsequently been estimated that 'khaki' (soldiers) and 'Jack Tar' (sailors) weddings accounted for perhaps three-quarters of all marriages in the city in 1915.

Reporting on the scene at the registrar's office in St Giles Ward, the *Scotsman*'s reporter may even have been present at Beatson and Carrie's wedding ceremony:

> [One] of the outstanding features of the war, so far as it affects the social life of the community, [is] that the present troubled times have witnessed something like a boom in matrimony. On many days during the past year the scene from the office of St Giles Ward has been an animated one. The number of people anxious to have their marriages registered or making inquiries regarding the procedure which has to be followed has on occasions been so large that some have had to stand outside the doors.

Soldiers and sailors have rubbed shoulders. . . . Military men who were old friends have met unexpectedly . . . and the more serious business [of having their weddings registered] is mixed with what is to several probably a more interesting and congenial occupation – relating their respective experiences at the battle front. Soldiers on leave for a few days from the war have seized the opportunity of getting married; others have seen to their matrimonial affairs just before leaving for the foreign field. Straight from the trenches to the registrar's office or direct from the office to the front will be the never-fading memory of some soldier benedicts of the past year.[81]

## Return to the Front – Death at High Wood

Beatson returned from leave in time to spend his first – and only – Christmas in the trenches. Unlike the previous year, however, there would be no informal truce, no games of football or exchanges of cigarettes in no-man's-land. Fraternisation with the enemy had been forbidden by the British High Command lest the Army's resolve be lessened by such contact with German soldiers, who were also flesh and bone and not the hideous creatures caricatured in British newspapers through lurid tales of torture and other atrocities. Indeed, the generals purposely prevented Tommies from developing the same empathy for their enemy as Beatson had for Heinrich.

The period until early July 1916 would later be described as 'more uneventful than any other similar period' in the history of the 9th Royal Scots.[82] Lieutenant Colonel Blair concluded the regimental war diary for December 1915 by noting that: 'The weather was very broken and a lot of work was done on the repair and drainage of fire and communication trenches. The health of the Battalion was satisfactory and the morale good.'

During January 1916 the Ninth moved from Bois de Vaux to, briefly, Suzanne, and then to Baizieux and finally Bertrancourt.

Casualties amounted to 2 killed, 13 wounded, and 1 missing. The two deaths occurred when the Germans shelled Suzanne on 11 January. The regimental war diary for January concluded in a similar vein to the previous month: 'The weather was comparatively dry, with no frost, and mild. The health of the Battalion was good and the morale excellent.'

February saw the Ninth move on to Beauquesne, with detachments at work in various villages in the Somme region. The battalion suffered no casualties. On 1 March 1916 the battalion assembled at Pierregot and joined the 154th Infantry Brigade of the 51st Division. After a few days training, including special classes for Lewis gunners, snipers, signallers and grenadiers, the battalion moved on to Etrun via Doullens, Ivergny and Maroueil. On 10 March it reached Etrun, 5 miles west of Arras. Two days later Beatson was promoted from Lance Corporal to Corporal. On the evening of 16 March the battalion relieved the 7th Battalion, Argyll & Sutherland Highlanders, A and B Companies occupying the front-line trenches, with C Company in support and D Company in reserve. The regimental war diary records:

> The fire trenches and communication trenches were left in very bad repair by the French and an enormous amount of work was done in cleaning them, making the parapet bullet proof, making firesteps and traverses, putting the fire trenches in repair and making a new first line and support line. Lewis gun emplacements and sniping posts were also made.

The battalion manned the trenches until relieved on the night of 22/23 March but returned to the trenches on the night of 28/29 March for another five days. During this period in the trenches casualties were higher than at any time since the Second Battle of Ypres: 6 dead and 18 wounded. During April the Ninth spent a further ten days in the trenches, and 11 men were wounded. The following month, however, casualties were heavier, with 4 dead and 30 injured as a result of the battalion spending fourteen days in the trenches. In June a further fourteen days in the front-line trenches saw 7 men of the Ninth killed and 31 wounded. In addition, on the night of 23/24 June one man was captured by the Germans following an enemy raid on one of the battalion's advanced sentry groups.

On 13 July, after a further five days in the trenches, the battalion marched to Chelers; a week later it moved on to Méaulte. The following day, 21 July, the men marched through Fricourt and Mametz and took over the front line near Bazentin-le-Grand Wood. From there they could see High Wood for the first time.

Beatson lost his life at High Wood on 23 July 1916 during the third week of the Battle of the Somme. Contrary to accounts published elsewhere, Sergeant Bill Hay was in A Company and did not take part in the attack on that day. But he later gave the following account of the fighting at High Wood involving B and C Companies of the Ninth:

> That was a stupid action, because we had to make a frontal attack on bristling German guns and there was no shelter at all. We were at the back, but B Company really got wiped out. We had a lot of casualties but they lost all their officers, all the NCOs, the lot – cleaned out! We knew it was pointless, even before we went over – crossing the open ground like that. But, you had to go. You were between the devil and the deep blue sea. If you go forward, you'll likely be shot. If you go back, you'll be court-martialled and shot. So what the hell do you do? What can you do? You just go forward, because the only bloke you can get your knife into is the bloke you're facing. There were dead bodies all over the place where previous battalions and regiments had taken part in previous attacks. What a bashing we got. There were heaps of men, everywhere – not one or two men, but heaps of men, all dead. Even before we went over, we knew this was death. We just couldn't take High Wood against machine-guns. It was ridiculous. There was no need for it. It was just absolute slaughter.[83]

Into this maelstrom we must imagine Beatson, now a seasoned veteran twice promoted, advancing. He knew what lay ahead, the piles of dead bodies from previous attempts remaining a visible and odorous reminder to all who followed after. As Beatson said in his diary, he was 'on easy terms with death', as were many soldiers inured to its daily visitations. But he could not have been comfortable with the astonishing power that can be wrought on flesh by red-hot metal. The wait was always the worst. As the indomitable Harry Patch, the last surviving soldier to have gone over the top, said, 'Any man who says he wasn't scared before going over the top is a damn liar.'

Only fools are unmoved by an imminent and potentially hideous wounding or an agonising, lingering death, and James Beatson was no fool. Fear is a natural emotion for soldiers, but the greatest concern they generally hold is that of losing their nerve and letting down their comrades. And then came the whistle. Perhaps Beatson was praying; perhaps he was busy ensuring his men did not bunch up; or perhaps he was overwhelmed by the horrific sights and overpowering stench of the battlefield – very likely all three. Beatson, a Royal Scot to the end, let no man down and died doing his duty for King and Country. Let no person say his death was a waste for then, by definition, they deny his sacrifice. He died for his cause and that should suffice us.

> I shall never forget the moment when we had to leave the shelter of the trenches. It is, indeed, terrible, the first step you take – right in the face of the most deadly fire and to realise that any moment you may be shot down; but if you are not hit, then you seem to gather courage and when you see, on either side of you, men like yourself, it inspires you with a determination to press forward.[84]

The entry in the regimental war diary for the Ninth records the events of the night of 22 July 1915 and the following day:

> The XIII, XV & III Corps continued the attack. The objective of the 51st Division was North East and North West edges of High Wood. . . . Front allotted to 9th Royal Scots was S 4 a.1.8

– M 33 d.40[85]. 4th Gordon Highlanders were on right.

Infantry assault began at 1.30 a.m. B&C Companies carried out the attack . . . Major J. Ferguson commanded B Company . . . Major R.H.F. Moncrieff commanded C Company . . . The assaulting companies were subjected to heavy shell fire while crossing open ground, also to machine-gun fire on reaching S 3.d. The two companies lost touch with each other and also with the battalions on right and left.

Major Moncrieff . . . [was] wounded and brought back . . . Major Ferguson . . . [was] also hit. Many of the NCOs and men became casualties, and the remainder of the two companies, having become split up, returned to the trench from which they had started. Major Ferguson . . . [was] found to be missing. The Battalion remained in original position.

Casualty return, in addition to [the eleven] Officers noted above, noon 22nd to noon 23rd. Killed 7 other ranks; wounded 89 other ranks; missing 66 other ranks.

In the evening the battalion was relieved by the 7th Battalion, Argyll & Sutherland Highlanders.

In all, during the month of July 1916 26 men of the Ninth, Beatson included, were killed, 150 wounded and 39 missing or taken prisoner. Beatson's body, along with an estimated eight thousand others, lies where it fell, cut down by German machine-guns as the 9th Royal Scots went 'over the top' before sunrise on that early July morning in 1916.

Although the popular belief is that the life expectancy of a 'Tommy' on the front line was as little as three weeks, this was only true of certain regiments at specific times during the war. From landing at Le Havre to his death in the battle for High Wood, Beatson survived 15 months on the Western Front, about the average for a British front-line infantry private and NCO.

One postscript. The British field guns had difficulty supporting the attacks on High Wood because they had to fire over Bazentin

Ridge. The low elevation of the guns meant the shells were just skimming over the British trenches and the margin for error was small, resulting in numerous casualties from 'friendly fire'. The possibility that this gifted young man's life was curtailed by 'friendly fire' makes its ending all the more tragic.

On 30 August 1916 the *Edinburgh Evening News* recorded the Official Roll:

> The casualty list issued by the War Office today contains the following names:
>
> KILLED
>
> ROYAL SCOTS – Corpl J.N. Beatson (2024), Edinburgh

The site where Beatson was killed, High Wood, is the only significant part of the Somme battlefield where the bodies of the fallen of both sides have never been recovered, on account of the high quantity of unexploded ordnance. James Nicol Beatson is remembered on Lutyens' imposing Memorial to the Missing of the Somme at Thiepval in France (pier 6D, face 7D).

### Beatson's Comrades

And what fate befell Beatson's friends and comrades, those he mentions in his diary?

In the event of his death, two men, William Swan and Cecil Valentine, were entrusted with returning Beatson's diary to his father. Private Swan (No. 2283) was transferred from the Ninth to the Army Service Corps as a lance-corporal (no. M/398004) and appears to have survived the war. More can be said about Private Valentine (No. 2358) who enlisted in September 1914, just a few days after Beatson. On 25 November 1915, in an article entitled 'Patriotic Leith Family', the *Scotsman* reported the major contribution being made to the war effort by Valentine's family. Two of his brothers, Corporal John and Lance-Corporal George, served with him in the 9th Royal Scots. His other brother, Gunner Harry, was in the Forth Royal Garrison Artillery. One of his brothers-in-law served with the Naval Air Squadron in the north of France, the other was involved in minesweeping off the south coast of England; one cousin was a member of the 3rd Battalion, Highland Light Infantry, another a Red Cross nurse serving in Serbia. Valentine himself was wounded during the Second Battle of Ypres in May 1915 and again during the Battle of the Somme in July 1916, but returned to action on both occasions. Tragically, he died on 10 June 1917 of wounds received two months earlier at the Battle of Arras; he was then aged only 19, but had been promoted to lance-corporal. He is buried at Galashiels (Eastlands) Cemetery (plot S1.17). Valentine's brothers and other relatives appear to have survived the war.

On 3 March 1915 Beatson and Swan enjoyed coffee and beer in a café in L'Abeele with 'Bill J.'. This may have been Private William C. Jamieson (No. 4365), who was killed in action on the Somme a month after Beatson, on 18 August 1916. Jamieson's body, like Beatson's, was not recovered from the Somme battlefield; he is commemorated at the Ploegsteert Memorial (panel 1), 8 miles south of Ypres.

On 23 March, while the battalion was stationed at Dickebusch and experiencing its first front-line fighting, Beatson detailed the fate of many of his comrades, remarking 'My heart is sore for the lads and their folks. God pity us.' He mourned the death of Sergeant Thomas Chrichton (No. 27), 'the first of our battalion to go west'. Sergeant Chrichton, from South Leith in Edinburgh, is commemorated on the Menin Gate (panel 11) at Ypres. On the same date Beatson recorded: 'Sergeant Thompson was good enough to compliment me on my work on Friday last.' Five years his senior, Sergeant Dugald Thompson died fighting alongside Beatson at High Wood on 23 July 1916. He is buried at Caterpillar Valley Cemetery, Longueval (XI.A.39), a few hundred yards south-east of High Wood.

Also on 23 March Beatson noted 'we have been having it pretty hot at times . . . Dryburgh [shot] on the forehead'. Regimental war diaries rarely mention any soldiers other than officers by name, yet the

Ninth's regimental war diary recorded Private J. Dryburgh (No. 2248) as being wounded while B Company, in two reliefs of 60, were putting up wire entanglements near St Eloi. This may have been a 'Blighty' wound as he survived the war.

Beatson also recorded how 'young Bennett fell, hit in the forehead two paces in front of me. Just a flutter and another lad gone west.' Aged 21, Private Frederick Ernest Bennett (No. 2268) was killed by a German sniper. He is buried at Elzenwalle Brasserie Cemetery (I.C.4), 3 miles south-west of Ypres.

Finally in that day's entry, Beatson wrote: 'I heard that Macdonald was hit in the breast today. His sergeant tells me he died soon after. I'm on easy terms with death but it's damnable to be hit in the dark by a sniping cur.' Private John William Scott MacDonald (No. 1991) was seriously wounded by a German sniper on 22 March 1915 at St Eloi and, contrary to what Beatson was told, eventually succumbed twelve days later, aged 19, in a hospital in Boulogne. He is buried at Boulogne Eastern Cemetery (III.D.74). In his melancholy state Beatson perhaps considered it superfluous to mention that his family and MacDonald's lived at the same address, for Private MacDonald's medal record card states that he was the son of John and Agnes MacDonald, of 22 Downfield Place, Edinburgh.

On 30 March Beatson mentioned that one of the French soldiers he met in a café 'gave me his rosary as a keepsake'. As far as we can ascertain from a search of French war records, this soldier, Sergeant Allouis Julien, survived the war.

On 10 April Beatson recorded: 'Watson and I led Lieutenant Smith-Grant up to Trench 73 last night and back again while the rest of the section replaced the casualties in C Company.' Lieutenant John Gordon Smith-Grant later transferred to the Royal Flying Corps (70 Squadron) and was killed in action on 30 May 1918. He is buried at Bagneux British Cemetery (III.A.7), Gezaincourt, 18 miles south-west of Arras.

On 13 April: 'while having breakfast about 6 o'clock Scott . . . [was] hit in the head by a sniper. Jock was also hit in the hand.' Private

Robert James Scott (No. 2510) died of wounds on 8 April 1915, aged 20. He is buried at Ramparts Cemetery (G.8) at Lille Gate in Ypres.

On 29 April: 'Bill Swan, Percy Telford and I lay under a pine tree and recalled bygone days of happiness spent in the country.' Private Percy Telford (No. 2896) enlisted with the Ninth in December 1914. He survived the war.

On 12 May: 'Poor Jimmy Smith killed yesterday in neighbouring traverse, on the eve of his discharge, the circumstances are particularly sad.' Private James Smith (No. 2033) was killed in action on 11 May 1915, aged 18. He is buried in Sanctuary Wood Cemetery (V.E.16), 2 miles east of Ypres.

Later that month Beatson wrote: 'a shadow is over our spirits as poor Bill Whitlie has just been carried away dead, shot through the head'. Private William J. Whitlie (No. 1679) was shot dead by a German sniper on 22 May 1915, aged 20, and is also buried at Sanctuary Wood Cemetery (V.E.23).

On 14 September: 'Farquharson was shot dead the other night.' Private Alexander McNaughton Farquharson (No. 1390) was killed by a German sniper on 12 September 1915, aged 21. He is buried at Ration Farm Military Cemetery, La Chapelle d'Armentières (VI.D.52), 11 miles south of Ypres, 8 miles west of Lille.

One man whom Beatson admired, perhaps loved, as only fellow, seasoned soldiers can, was Sergeant Alexander Mitchell (No. 3/6825) of the 10th Battalion, Gordon Highlanders,[86] who was mentioned in the diary on 10 May, 1 June ('he looks bronzed and brawny') and 9 June. However, four months later on 12 October Beatson wrote in distress: 'Alick, dear, dear Alick, staunch and true, generous, open as the day. I loved you as a brother and would gladly have given myself in your place. Never will I meet your like again, never will I forget you, never will I mourn you as I ought. May God count me worthy to meet you again, dear, dear brother of mine, Alick.' Sergeant Mitchell is buried in Fosse 7 Military Cemetery (also known as 'Quality Street'), Mazingarbe (I.B.7); he was killed in action on 23 September 1915.

**Beatson's Family**
The violent and sudden loss of any close and much-loved family member is always a destructive and devastating event, perhaps more so if that individual is of the kindly, godly and sensitive disposition that James possessed. His father John never recovered from the loss and in his twilight years, with his mind perhaps wandering, would frequently ask after his son. Though he served again in the Second World War, it was naturally on the home front. After 1945 he went to live with his eldest daughter and her only child, May, born in 1922. Bella had married shortly after the war and was now Mrs Isabella Beatson Robinson. For a short while Carrie lived with them too until she married again in 1924, much to the consternation of the Beatson family, who let contact with her drift into silence. James's younger brother Donald perished in a vat of molten metal, and five of his remaining nine uncles and aunts moved to Canada and a sixth to Australia. Bella's daughter May had a daughter who sadly died in middle age but was able to bless May with five grandchildren, four of whom now live in Australia. May sold James's diary in order to finance the education of her grandchild still in England. She is currently top of her class in her final year studying law.

James's diary, however, had another act of drama to perform (aside from, we hope, raising significant funds for two worthy charities), as his words resulted in the closing of a long-broken circle. As a result of researching James's family, both William's and John's heirs were contacted by the editors. As a result of these contacts it was suggested that perhaps the two sides of the family, apart for over a century owing to a long-forgotten argument, might wish to renew their kindred ties. William Beatson (Uncle William's great-grandson) spoke with May in 2008. May, then a sprightly and alert 86 years young and living pretty much alone in the West Country, was delighted to discover from William she had a long-lost relative just 10 miles down the road. And so James's words have brought his family back together again.

**In Memoriam**

On 20 October Beatson quoted the Belgian poet Leon Montenaeken, who was evidently well known to him and whose works he liked sufficiently to commit to memory. In his diary entry, in the third line of the poem he substitutes 'peine' (pain) instead of 'haine' (hatred). A fitting end.

> La vie est vaine,
> Un peu d'amour,
> Un peu de haine,
> Et puis – bonjour!
> La vie est brève,
> Un peu d'espoir,
> Un peu de rêve,
> Et puis – bonsoir!
> *Life is vain,*
> *A little love,*
> *A little hate,*
> *And then – good day!*
> *Life is short,*
> *A little hope,*
> *A little dream,*
> *And then – goodnight!*[87]

# A Note on the Photographs

Official war photography did not start until early 1916, when the first official photographer was appointed and the British Army started to enforce strictly – at least for privates, less so for officers – the ban on amateur photography by soldiers. Therefore, photographs of the actual events of 1915 described by Private Beatson are relatively rare. For example, of the many millions of photographs preserved in the Imperial War Museum's incredible archive, only two are of the 9th Royal Scots from around Beatson's time: at rest in Leith, Scotland in 1914, and marching on the Amiens-Albert Road in 1916. Both are reproduced in this book. Consequently, the other photographs we have included to illustrate Private Beatson's diary are indicative of the life he experienced in the trenches and of the events he witnessed. By coincidence, a number of them feature soldiers from other Scottish regiments, such as the Argyll and Sutherland Highlanders and Royal Scots Fusiliers, as well as the London Scottish.

The vast majority of the photographs are from the archive of the Imperial War Museum, London and we are indebted to Yvonne Oliver, Licensing Manager, for kindly permitting us to reproduce these free of charge on account of the charitable purpose of this book. We are also grateful to have sourced a number of images from the archive of our publisher, Pen & Sword, which includes the Taylor Library. Despite their age, the photographs are generally preserved in excellent condition; for a handful of images we applied a small amount of digital retouching to repair scratched negatives.

Some of the photographs, such as those showing the Argyll and Sutherland Highlanders wearing primitive gas masks, are rightly considered to be iconic images of the war. Although they have been reproduced in many publications over the years, their ability to evoke both incredulity as to the conditions faced by soldiers on the Western Front, and gratitude for the bravery with which they endured them, remains to this day.

Some other photographs, either less often seen or published possibly for the first time, are no less resonant. The sight of German soldiers imperiously crossing the Belgian countryside and of Belgian soldiers preparing to defend one of the roads leading to Antwerp illustrate the early stages of the war before the stalemate of trench warfare set in. We must thank our publisher for agreeing to include more photographic plates than had been originally intended, thus enabling us to show such a wide range of illustrations.

We are indebted also to Colonel R.P. Mason, Regimental Secretary of the Royal Scots Museum at Edinburgh Castle, for permission to use the photograph of the 9th Royal Scots crossing the English Channel aboard HMT *Inventor*. Though not such a high-quality photograph as some of the others, it captures perfectly the cramped conditions in which Beatson and his comrades were transported, like cattle, to the theatre of war.

Most significantly, we were fortunate enough to obtain from Beatson's remarkable niece, May Beatson, three treasured photographs: of Beatson with his mother, brother and sister; of Beatson's father; and a portrait of Beatson himself that also adorns the cover of this book.

Right up to the last minute as we prepared the book for publication photographs were still coming to our attention that we felt compelled to use. One such is the picture of four men of the Ninth shaving, or at least pretending to shave, with their bayonets, illustrating a nice sense of humour among Beatson's comrades. For this image, we are indebted to George Souness. This picture, along with others of the Royal Scots and other Scottish regiments, can be found on the excellent Newbattle at War website (www.freewebs.com/eltoro1960) set up by John Duncan and dedicated to men from Midlothian who fought in the

Great War. We are grateful also to Mike Insall of the Hampshire Air-Sea Photo Library for permission to use his aerial photograph of High Wood as it is today. We first came across this image on Alan Jennings' excellent website, www.ww1battlefields.co.uk.

Finally, we chose to accompany the photographs with excerpts from Beatson's diary, not to trivialise the images in any way, but to emphasise their link with the events he witnessed.

Stuart Humphreys and Shaun Springer

# *Notes*

1. Having been first elected as a Conservative MP in October 1900, Churchill switched to the Liberal Party in May 1904 because of Tory opposition to Free Trade. After years of increasing mutual disenchantment, Churchill left the Liberals in December 1923 when they allowed Labour to form its first ever government. After Tory leader Stanley Baldwin renounced protectionism, the pro-Free Trade Churchill returned to the Conservative Party and was elected as a Tory MP in 1924.
2. 'Colonel Blair on the "Dandy Ninth"', *Scotsman*, 19 July 1915.
3. 'Reception to the 9th Royal Scots', *Scotsman*, 16 February 1915.
4. Ibid.
5. Ibid.
6. Ibid.
7. *9th Royal Scots (T.F.) B Company on Active Service*, pp. 8–9.
8. Ibid., p. 10.
9. Princess Patricia's Canadian Light Infantry. In early 1915 the PPCLI pioneered trench raids, the aim of which was to capture German prisoners and documents in order to obtain military intelligence.
10. '9th Royal Scots in action', *Edinburgh Evening News*, 1 May 1915.
11. *9th Royal Scots (T.F.) B Company on Active Service*, p. 64.
12. 'The Gallantry of the "Ninth"', *Edinburgh Evening News*, 5 May 1915.
13. *9th Royal Scots (T.F.) B Company on Active Service*, p. 63.
14. 'Stories from the battlefield', *Scotsman*, 8 June 1915.
15. Letter from J.L. Ferrier, *Scotsman*, 14 November 1914.

16. 'Comforts for Scottish soldiers in the field', *Scotsman*, 8 June 1915.
17. Ibid.
18. 'Impressions of life at the Front', *Scotsman*, 18 May 1915.
19. 'News of the 9th Royal Scots', *Scotsman*, 16 March 1915.
20. '"Dandy Ninth's" mails: a favoured battalion', *Edinburgh Evening News*, 29 March 1915.
21. 'A Night with the Dandy Ninth', *Edinburgh Evening News*, 1 April 1915.
22. 'Edinburgh territorials killed in France', *Scotsman*, 14 April 1915.
23. 'The Gallantry of the "Ninth"', *Edinburgh Evening News*, 5 May 1915.
24. Ibid.
25. *9th Royal Scots (T.F.) B Company on Active Service*, p. 49.
26. Ibid, p. 50.
27. Ibid, p. 51.
28. 'The Gallantry of the "Ninth"', *Edinburgh Evening News*, 5 May 1915.
29. *9th Royal Scots (T.F.) B Company on Active Service*, pp. 51–2.
30. 'The Gallantry of the "Ninth"', *Edinburgh Evening News*, 5 May 1915.
31. Ibid.
32. '9th Royal Scots in action', *Edinburgh Evening News*, 1 May 1915.
33. 'The Gallantry of the "Ninth"', *Edinburgh Evening News*, 5 May 1915.
34. *9th Royal Scots (T.F.) B Company on Active Service*, pp. 61–2.
35. Ibid, p. 64.
36. Ibid, p. 81.
37. 'Colonel Blair on the "Dandy Ninth"', *Scotsman*, 19 July 1915.
38. Modern-day Thessaloniki in Greece.
39. *9th Royal Scots (T.F.) B Company on Active Service*, p. 9.
40. Ibid, p. 10.
41. Probably a reference to the 'Ligue Nationale Contre l'Alcoolisme', formed from a number of groups in the pre-war period, when the

temperance movement was particularly strong in France. The old lady to whom Beatson refers would be the head of a local branch of the league, which particularly targeted soldiers during the war and tried to get women on board in fighting the good fight.

42. Acting as a guide was a dangerous job. By early 1915 both sides were aware that troop movements took place at night and had the communication trenches' coordinates pinpointed for attention. In addition, it often meant crouching to pass numerous German sniper points along the front-line trenches. Leaving aside the danger from shelling, it was extremely tiring and a thankless task. If the guide managed to find the correct drop-off point, then so be it; but woe betide the poor soldier who got himself and his followers lost. However, the duty did bring some benefits such as days off, release from fatigues and an extra tot of rum on occasion.

43. An ancient abbey founded in 1057 and close to the Messines ridge.

44. This moment is also described 'by a private anonymous soldier' in Lyn Macdonald's *1915: The Death of Innocence*, pp. 188–9.

45. Major J. Ewing MC, *The Royal Scots 1914–1919*, p. 90.

46. Possibly an oblique reference to the 'splendid isolation' description of Britain's foreign policy in the late nineteenth century regarding its lack of involvement in European affairs. The *Entente Cordiale* and other political alliances formed in the early part of the twentieth century would mark an end to this policy and ultimately ensure Britain's involvement in the war following Germany's invasion of neutral Belgium.

47. Although shooting oneself in the foot would normally be a court-martial offence, there is no record of any members of the Ninth being court-martialled during this period.

48. At the time of writing this entry, neither the second nor the third battles of Ypres had yet taken place, although the former was less than a fortnight off.

49. As indeed was the case. The Germans had decided to focus their attention on the Eastern Front. The forthcoming gas attack was meant as nothing more than a test of the effectiveness of this new

weapon but little was expected by the German High Command. That they nearly broke through illustrates both the shock value of gas when it was initially used and the chaos wrought by its effects. That the Germans did not break through is a testament to the fortitude of the mainly Canadian troops opposing them, the military acumen of the commanders on the ground, and the slowness of the Germans to seize the opportunity.

50. The Germans were in reality ranging their guns while awaiting a change in the wind direction. The gain of Hill 60 by the British was reported in the German press as involving the first use of gas, and was subsequently used by the Germans as their justification for using gas a week later. In attempting to justify this infringement of the rules of war, the German War Ministry and High Command in 1917 charged the French Army with having used a rifle grenade filled with bromic acid, and a hand grenade filled with ethyl bromo-acetate liquid. The German Official History brands the French use of gas shells and gas hand grenades from the end of February 1915 as 'the first breach of international agreement in the sphere of gas warfare'. Interestingly, the Hague agreements had barred the use of such projectiles only when their *sole* objective was the diffusion of asphyxiating gases. 'The Battles of Ypres which began on April 22nd', states the Reichsarchiv, 'had their origin on the German side solely in the desire to trial a new weapon, gas, thoroughly at the front.'

51. Presumably Miss Alston is related to John Alston, Beatson's best man at his wedding in December 1915.

52. Beatson is referring to the 'black' Algerian Zouaves who raised nine *regiments de marche* for France and were noted for their panache in attack. Arguably the Algerians had the most splendidly colourful uniforms of the war. Without question, the variety and colours of the French army uniforms gave the French soldiers the dubious accolade of being the most 'chic' casualties on the fields of Alsace and Lorraine. The French, in fact, were still embedded in the *En Avant* and *L'Attacke* philosophy upheld by their

Commander in Chief, General Joffre.

53. As no diagram is drawn in the diary, it would seem a loose leaf was inserted here and subsequently lost, or it was intended to be inserted at a later date. We have mentioned this entry in the Introduction as being one of the pieces of evidence that the diary was not a rewritten work.

54. This rather banal entry masks the reality of the situation in which the British line was very nearly broken save for a celebrated series of actions. A mixed force of a few half battalions and the odd company had been cobbled together by General Geddes and thrown into the line. Had the Germans continued their movement they would have found this embryonic defence easily brushed aside with no reserve line to hinder them thereafter. In the event, the Germans were so surprised by their advance that they halted to await the arrival of their heavy artillery.

55. The British had just lost Frezenberg Ridge under terrific shelling.

56. By being asked to 'hold this line', Beatson and his comrades were in effect being asked to hold the line 'to the last man', a great compliment indeed and one that emphasised the gravity of the situation.

57. As if Beatson's diary were not extraordinary enough, this and a few of the preceding and subsequent entries are nothing less than 'live' journalism. Events that were actually taking place when these words were penned travel, with an immortal timelessness, through to the present, allowing the reader to enter this soldier's war. How many other literary works concerning warfare have been written not just during the battle but whilst in the thick of it?

58. Beatson is probably remarking on the Battle of Festubert, launched by the British on 15 May. It was a success, with the British taking Festubert and consolidating it on 17 May.

59. Beatson is referring to the German attacks on Festubert on 23 May and east of Ypres on 24 May, both of which were repulsed with heavy casualties to both sides.

60. Beatson naturally did not know that the term 'Kitchener's Army'

would later be used to refer to the volunteer army that was assembled during 1914 and 1915 and, aside from the Territorials, did not see action until 1916. As Secretary of State for War, Kitchener was effectively the head of the army, George V aside, and hence Beatson's reference to 'Kitchener's Army'.

61. Although it is impossible to prove, it would seem that Beatson wrote this entry while 'one over the eight'. The handwriting is certainly less disciplined in its appearance and the abandoned gaiety of this passage indicates a state of mind not hitherto seen in the diary. His meeting with Claude (probably 'Claudette') seems to have been less than platonic. What strikes one most is his sheer joy in being alive. It is an endearing though somewhat disjointed section of the diary that nevertheless affords the reader a glimpse of the emotions of a soldier at war.

62. Irwin Cobb was an American reporter most noted for his reports from the front during 1914 and 1915 from behind the German lines. His heavily censored reports were viewed by Allied soldiers as unrealistically sanitised; in fact, this was an unjust accusation but perhaps an understandable one from the perspective of those in the trenches.

63. Hereon the writing reverts to its usual disciplined appearance.

64. A national French daily newspaper, reinforcing the impression that Beatson was fully conversant in French as well as possessing a fairly decent Latin vocabulary; a later diary entry sees him reading German as well – see note 80 below.

65. It appears that Beatson had intended to make an entry but was possibly diverted by a tour of inspection by General Sir Douglas Haig, referred to as 'a general rode past' in the next day's entry.

66. Beatson is paraphrasing 'Sergius' from Shaw's most memorable play. The setting of *Arms and the Man* is war-torn Bulgaria, and the play focuses not only on the romance between the young people of the cast, but also on the atrocities that are practised during times of war and the ability of ordinary people to turn a blind eye to them. Germany still to this day is debating with itself

on this same topic, as indeed are the French. First produced in 1894, Shaw's play turned out to be sadly prophetic. When war was declared, young men flooded into the recruitment offices carrying with them the same romantic – and wholly inaccurate – ideas of the 'glories' of war that Raina and her mother Catherine uphold at the beginning of the play. Over the drama's course, Raina loses her romantic perfectionism to reveal a more actual, creative and accurate version that allows her to find true love. Sergius, her betrothed, after going through a similar transformation, realises that there must be more to himself than the two-dimensional ideal of the soldier that young ladies seem to worship.

67. Juho Pietari 'Hannes' Kolehmainen (1889–1966) was a Finnish long-distance runner, one of the original 'Flying Finns'. A star of the 1912 Summer Olympics in Stockholm, winning three gold medals, he went on to win gold in the marathon at the first post-war Olympics in Antwerp in 1920.

68. From late July, through August and into September Kitchener's new army, over 120,000 strong, was arriving in France. The Battle of Loos began on 25 September. Beatson's demand for unconditional surrender, born from the conviction he so eloquently describes, is a sentiment common to soldiers throughout history. Their expectation that politicians would betray them is best illustrated in a post-war German soldier's book, *Mein Kampf*.

69. A quite exemplary description: Pulteney is the image of a de-spectacled Captain Mainwaring of *Dad's Army* fame. It seems fair to say that General Pulteney was not highly regarded. His chief of staff described him as 'completely ignorant' and fellow officers nicknamed him 'Putty', evidently a comment on what he had between his ears. That said, Pulteney's visits to the Ninth in August and September were much appreciated, particularly his comments regarding the excellent conduct of the battalion.

70. The General Staff comprised some 650 elite officers who served

as the 'brains' and 'nerve centre' of the German army. The prefix 'Great' had been applied to the general staff of the Prussian army since the unification of Germany in 1871, to distinguish it from those of Bavaria, Saxony and Württemberg.

71. The word 'English' appears thus quoted by Beatson. The world did not differentiate between England and Britain, which were essentially synonymous.

72. General Friedrich von Bernhardi's ideas did not correspond with the official views of the Kaiser's government or even with those of the General Staff but they were fully in keeping with those of extreme nationalists in the Pan-German League. According to such men, war was a right and a duty, a biological imperative sanctioned by the findings of Darwin.

73. A booming business was developing back in Britain with charlatans preying on hapless widows. Sir Arthur Conan Doyle and Rudyard Kipling both had sons who died in the war. John Kipling was destined to die within a month of this diary entry. While heartbroken wives and mothers (they were generally women) needed little encouragement to pursue this spurious means of contacting their lost ones, the fact that it was later advocated by Conan Doyle and participated in by Kipling's wife did little to undermine this sharp practice.

74. 'Three times three' is the basic three-gun salute, with three salvos from three members of the regiment.

75. The Royal Scots were among the first regiments to arrive in the Somme area when the British extended their line at French insistence.

76. From the *Rougon-Macquart* cycle, a massive forty-volume work by Zola that Beatson appears to have read in its entirety.

77. A reference to one of the poems in Robert Louis Stevenson's collection *A Child's Garden of Verses*, published in 1885.

78. Sir John Moore commanded the British forces in the Iberian Peninsula from 1803 until his death at Corunna in 1810. It is quite possible that Beatson had read *The Recollections of Rifleman*

*Harris*, which is considered to be one of the greatest diaries written by a member of the PBI (Poor Bloody Infantry).

79. Here Beatson quotes from a poem in French by the Belgian poet Leon Montenaeken, substituting the word 'peine' (pain) for 'heine' (hate). The poem is quoted in full at the end of the Epilogue.

80. A German trench magazine, suggesting the possibility that Beatson could also read German.

81. '"Khaki weddings" – remarkable increase in marriages in Edinburgh', *Scotsman*, 29 December 1915.

82. Major J. Ewing MC, *The Royal Scots 1914–1919*, p. 256.

83. From the diary of Sergeant William (Bill) Hay.

84. From the diary of Private Ridley Scott, C Company, 6th Battalion, Manchesters; he managed just 20 yards before being wounded in the leg.

85. Trench map coordinates.

86. Sergeant Alexander Mitchell was in the 8th Battalion, Gordon Highlanders according to Beatson.

87. George du Maurier's poem *A Life* bears a remarkable similarity. As both were contemporary poets it would be interesting to know whose was first published. Its first verse reads:

> A little work, a little play
> To keep us going
> And so – good-day!

And its fourth verse:

> A little trust that when we die
> We reap our sowing
> And so – good-bye!

# Bibliography

Anon, *9th Royal Scots (T.F.) B Company on Active Service, From a Private's Diary, February–May 1915* (Turnbull & Spears, 1916)

Corrigan, Gordon, *Mud, Blood and Poppycock* (Cassell, 2003)

Cross, Robin, *In Memoriam: Remembering the Great War* (Ebury Press, 2008)

Ewing, Major J., *The Royal Scots 1914–1919* (Oliver & Boyd, 1925)

Fromkin, David, *Europe's Last Summer: Who Started the Great War in 1914?* (Vintage Books, 2005)

Gilbert, Martin, *First World War* (Weidenfeld & Nicolson, 1994)

Hall Caine, Thomas Henry, *The Drama of 365 Days: Scenes in the Great War* (William Heinemann, 1915)

Holmes, Richard, *Tommy: The British Soldier on the Western Front 1914-1918* (HarperCollins, 2004)

Holmes, Richard, *Shots from the Front: The British Soldier 1914-1918* (Harper Press, 2008)

Macdonald, Lyn, *1915, The Death of Innocence* (Penguin Books, 1997)

Norman, Terry, *The Hell They Called High Wood: The Somme 1916* (Pen & Sword, repr. 2007)

Stone, Norman, *World War One: A Short History* (Allen Lane, 2007)

# Index